GAME OVER

GAME OVER

JERRY SANDUSKY,
PENN STATE, AND
THE CULTURE
OF SILENCE

Bill Moushey and Bob Dvorchak

WILLIAM MORROW
An Imprint of HarperCollins*Publishers*

HarperCollins books may be purchased for educational, business, or sales
promotional use. For information please write: Special Markets Department,
HarperCollins Publishers, 10 East 53rd Street, New York, NY 10022.

FIRST EDITION

Library of Congress Cataloging-in-Publication Data has been applied for.

ISBN 978-0-06-220113-3

12   13   14   15   16   DIX/RRD   10   9   8   7   6   5   4   3   2   1

Dedicated to the young men and their advocates who had the courage to speak out and who now know that they are not alone

CONTENTS

GAME OVER

PROLOGUE

The journey to Penn State University is challenging even when the weather is ideal. The drive from Philadelphia, two hundred miles to the east, or from Pittsburgh, a hundred fifty miles west, takes three hours and requires the crossing of mountain ridges and rivers to reach a campus situated in the middle of the state and seemingly in the middle of nowhere. The trip was even more arduous for Penn State football fans traveling there on October 29, 2011, because of a surprise snowstorm pummeling the northeast from Washington, D.C., to Maine. But this was a football Saturday tinged with history. Pilgrims making the trek to the game shared the roads with snowplows and salt trucks while keeping tabs on weather advisories. University officials alerted fans about the closure of grass-lot parking areas and scrambled to make shuttle buses available to service paved lots too far away to slog through six inches of snow to Beaver Stadium, where a 3:30 kickoff was scheduled.

Despite the headaches posed by the weather, the fans arriving in Happy Valley, the nickname of the idyllic setting surrounding the town of

State College, Pennsylvania, were in a festive mood. Coach Joe Paterno, a man revered by the Penn State faithful, was one game away from the 409th win of his career. A victory over Illinois, the opponent that day, would distinguish him as the winningest coach in the history of Division I college football.

Sixty-one years had passed since Paterno, an octogenarian, first set foot on campus in 1950, two years after Penn State played its last season in leather helmets. An outsider at first, the Brooklyn-born Paterno arrived as an assistant coach under Charles "Rip" Engle, who came to Penn State after coaching Paterno as a quarterback and defensive back at Brown University.

At Brown, Paterno majored in English literature and took courses preparing him for law school. With his thick-rimmed black glasses, he looked more like a professor than a play-caller. He was fond of quoting the English poet Robert Browning: "A man's reach should exceed his grasp, or what's a heaven for?" But football was in his blood, and he set down roots after falling in love with Penn State. When Engle retired in 1966, Paterno took over with an ambitious plan to make Penn State a football powerhouse by stressing academics and athletics. His blueprint came to be known as the "Grand Experiment."

Forty-six years after his first win in his first game, Paterno had become the face of Penn State. No other coach had built such all-encompassing power at one school and kept it for so long. No other coach had more winning seasons, more postseason appearances, and more bowl victories.

JoePa, as he was affectionately called, was already enshrined in the College Football Hall of Fame in South Bend, Indiana. Winning so much for so long made him seem larger than life, larger than the seven-foot-tall statue of him outside the university's football stadium. The monument includes his words: "They ask me what I'd like written about me when I'm gone. I hope they write I made Penn State a better place, not just that I was a good football coach."

Paterno's success had enriched the school as well. The coach had grown Penn State's football program into a moneymaker that turned a profit of $53 million a year, the third-largest moneymaking machine in college sports. The profits were enough to finance every other sports program at the university. Penn State's endowment was flush with cash from alumni donations, corporate sponsorships, and TV revenue. Beyond that, Paterno and his wife, Suzanne, a Penn State grad who majored in English literature and the matriarch of what she called the "Penn State family," had donated $4 million of their own money and helped raise $13.5 million more to fund a five-story expansion of the main library on campus. Suzanne had a legacy of her own: her name adorns the Suzanne Pohland Paterno Catholic Student Faith Center at the center of campus. Penn State may be the only university in the country where the library is named after the football coach and the football stadium is named after a former administrator. It made perfect sense at Penn State.

Approaching State College from any direction, one can see Beaver Stadium, a massive, imposing monolith as recognizable as Mount Nittany, the landmark geographic feature that dominates Happy Valley. With a capacity of 106,572, it is twice as large as the new Yankee Stadium in New York. In fact, it is the second-largest stadium in the Western Hemisphere and the fourth largest in the world. During Paterno's reign, the stadium was expanded six times and held double the number of fans from when he first became head coach. The latest expansion, completed in 2001 at a cost of $94 million, added 11,000 seats, including sixty high-end and enclosed skyboxes. The extra seats, however, caused some dismay for ticket buyers because new construction obscured the view of Mount Nittany for some inside the stadium.

Paterno and football were so popular that students arrived the night before a game, sometimes days before, to get in line for a crack at the choicest seats in the student section. These fanatics erected tents as shelter against the elements and unrolled sleeping bags on the concrete sidewalk outside the stadium. The encampment was called Paternoville, and students abided by rules of conduct established by the self-styled Paternoville Coordination Committee. To keep their spirits high, Coach Paterno was known to stop by with pizza from time to time. While the older alumni were more apt to bundle up in parkas and foul weather gear on a snowy Saturday, some occupants of Paternoville slathered their bare upper torsos with blue and white paint to show their team spirit, no matter how much dis-

comfort they had to endure. Others donned Paterno masks to pay homage
to the coach. Their wake-up call on this snowy Saturday was the whir of
snowblowers clearing the playing field. Grounds crews equipped with snow
shovels fought the battle in the seating areas.

Penn State players had a one-mile journey of their own to get to the stadium. They donned their uniforms at the Lasch Football Building, which
houses the locker rooms and showers and adjoins the fields where the team
practices during the week. Then they rode four blue university buses to the
arena. Fans lining the route shouted encouragement and waved Penn State
flags as the buses passed. At the main gate more fans formed a human
tunnel, so the players made a hero's entry through the cheering admirers
and into the packed stadium.

Because of the snowstorm, only an estimated 62,000 zealots occupied
the seats for the game against Illinois, which, like Penn State, competed in
the Big Ten Conference. Conforming with pregame tradition, fans rose to
sing the Penn State alma mater.

As the game got under way, Paterno watched the action from a glass-
enclosed viewing box high above the field. No longer did he prowl the sidelines during games; he was limited by shoulder and hip injuries incurred
when a player ran into him at a preseason practice the previous August.
Assistant coaches on the sidelines were handling the nitty-gritty chores associated with running today's game, aided by direction from Paterno. One
of those assistants, a State College native and former quarterback named
Mike McQueary, relayed plays from Paterno transmitted into his headset
and sent them into the offensive huddle.

Snowy conditions and sloppy play kept the teams scoreless in the first
half. Illinois had a 10–7 lead going into the final quarter, but Penn State
rallied and capped an eighty-yard drive to take its first lead with sixty-eight
seconds remaining. The Fighting Illini counterpunched and were in position to tie the score with a field goal. But as the game clock ticked down to
zero, Derek Dimke's forty-two-yard attempt caromed off the right upright.
The right bounce at the right time preserved the 10–7 lead. Game over.
Just as Zeus ruled the world from Mount Olympus, Joe Paterno reigned
supreme over the world of college football from Mount Nittany.

In a postgame ceremony that was broadcast from a media room to the fans remaining in the stadium, the coach was given a plaque that read, "Joe Paterno. Educator of Men. Winningest Coach. Division One Football." Making the presentation were the university's president Graham B. Spanier and athletic director Tim Curley. It was validation for Paterno in more ways than one. Seven years earlier he had had several meetings with Spanier and Curley about whether it was time for him to retire. At the time Penn State had languished through four losing seasons over a five-year span, a period that Penn Staters called the Dark Ages. Paterno thought about ending his storied career, but eventually decided to stay on to restore the program to its winning ways. When the time came for him to leave, he wanted to go out on his own terms.

After the brief ceremony, alumni returned to their blue-and-white recreational vehicles for their postgame tailgate parties. Having begun the day with morning mimosas, they now toasted Paterno's 409th victory with cocktails and beer. Students adjourned to the campus parties and taprooms along Beaver Avenue in State College, where beer flowed freely from numerous kegs. Paterno returned to his house on McKee Street for dinner with family and select friends.

One more laurel loomed on the horizon, and it was a significant one. By appearing in one more game, which was scheduled after a weekend off, Paterno would surpass the record for number of games coached, a milepost he currently shared with Amos Alonzo Stagg. Stagg was a college football pioneer at the University of Chicago, which was a charter member of the Big Ten Conference. The names of Stagg and Paterno were already etched together on the Big Ten's new championship trophy. With one more coaching appearance, Paterno could claim top billing. But he was never one to get ahead of himself; from lessons learned in literature and on the football field, he liked to say, "Just when you think you have it made, disaster is right around the corner."

This time he was right. A deep, dirty secret that had been festering in the muck for fifteen years would rise to the surface and explode before Paterno would get the chance to coach again. Over the past year, Paterno, along with Spanier, Curley, and McQueary, had testified before a statewide

grand jury investigating criminal complaints against one Jerry Sandusky.
A former Penn State football player, Sandusky had once been considered
Paterno's heir apparent, but he had retired suddenly in 1999. Paterno had
let him slip away without much fanfare, and Sandusky never sought a
job anywhere else, which seemed curious for such a celebrated talent. A
member of the coaching staff for thirty-two years, he had been the defensive coordinator in the two seasons culminating in national championships,
so most people found his retirement quite surprising. Even after his departure Sandusky could be found in the VIP section at almost every home
game. He and his wife, Dottie, had been seen happily socializing in an area
of the stadium reserved for those holding club and private box seats the day
the Nittany Lions had given Paterno his 409th victory.

Within a week, however, Sandusky would be arraigned on charges of
sexually abusing children under his care, and Joe Paterno would be fired,
accused of whitewashing knowledge he had of Sandusky's heinous behavior
on the grounds of Penn State University. The allegations, and rumors of an
alleged cover-up, were shocking. The legendary Paterno would never get
the chance to coach again.

The final verse of Penn State's alma mater, always sung with rousing
spirit right before kick off, is this:

May no act of ours bring shame
To one heart that loves thy name.
May our lives swell that fame,
Dear Old State, Dear Old State.

The acts of Jerry Sandusky and the inaction of Joe Paterno, Mike Mc-
Queary, and Tim Curley would ruin lives, damage the university, and dis-
lodge the peaceful isolation of Happy Valley.

CHAPTER ONE

BIRTH OF A LEGEND

The Friday afternoon shadows were lengthening as Charles "Rip" Engle drove his dark blue Cadillac onto the campus of Penn State University on May 26, 1950. He and his young passenger had started out before dawn from Providence, Rhode Island, for the 342-mile trip. Engle had just left his job as the head football coach at Brown University to take the same position at Penn State, and Joe Paterno, his travel mate and one of his star players was going to be his assistant coach. The two men were eager to see their new home field.

Engle, forty-four and already graying, was returning full circle to his native Pennsylvania. A no-nonsense, organized man who didn't smoke or drink, he had been a coach at the high school and college levels for twenty-one years, the previous six as head of the Brown University Bears. His new superiors at Penn State hoped he would bring some stability to a football program that had gone through four coaches in four years.

Engle was allowed to bring only one person to join him at Penn State. He was thrilled that young Joe Paterno had said yes. Joe, a native of Brook-

lyn, had just graduated from Brown and had already enrolled at Boston
University School of Law for the fall semester. His plan was to become a
lawyer like his father. But when Rip Engle dangled the prospect of an assistant coaching job at Penn State, Joe had decided to try it, telling his parents
he was going to save a little money for law school. Joe's mother, Florence,
had been heartbroken when he told her he was going to put law school on
hold for a career she thought was rather frivolous. She wanted him to practice law and maybe wear a judge's robe one day. She told him that he had
wasted his time going to college if he was just going to be a coach.

Joe's father, Angelo, also wasn't enamored with the idea, but he wanted
Joe to find his own path. The dark-haired twenty-three-year-old had been
Engle's star quarterback at Brown and had also played cornerback. This
would be his first real coaching job. Most of what he knew about the nuts
and bolts of coaching he had just learned from Engle on the five-hour drive
from Providence. He wasn't yet sold on coaching as a career, but when he
stepped out of Engle's Cadillac into his new surroundings, he felt at home.

Joe brought a lot of Brooklyn with him to pastoral Pennsylvania, starting with an accent delivered in a high, scratchy voice that sounded like the
screeching wheels of a New York subway train. He was born on December
21, 1926, the oldest of Angelo and Florence Cafiero Paterno's three children. The Paterno family made their home among the two-family dwellings,
row houses, and tenement apartments of Eighteenth Street in Brooklyn's
Flatbush neighborhood, and family meant everything to them.

Joe never tired of telling people that his grandfather, Vincente Paterno,
had crossed the Atlantic Ocean on a passenger ship in the 1890s. He even
mentioned his grandfather in his postgame news conference following his
409th win. Vincente was born in Cosenza, Italy, and found work in New
York as a barber to support his family. Joe's father was the man Joe respected most in life because he had worked and sacrificed for everything
he had. Angelo had dropped out of high school to join the army and fight
in France during World War I. After the armistice he returned to Flatbush
and worked by day to get his high school diploma at night. Then, while
working as a clerk in the Appellate Division of the New York State Supreme
Court, Angelo attended night school to become a lawyer. Joe remembered

the nights his father stayed up until three in the morning to study for the bar exam, which he had to pass in order to practice in the New York City court system.

Angelo taught his children to respect others. "He instilled in us the notion that religion shouldn't matter, color shouldn't matter. It didn't matter if you were Italian or Irish or Jewish or black, all that matters is what kind of person you are," Joe once told an audience of the NAACP. Angelo also taught his children to be forthright when they made a mistake. A problem would solve itself if it weren't compounded by a lie, he told them. A tireless worker, he somehow found time to play on a semipro football team that competed in the New York metropolitan area. He passed along that passion for football to Joe and his younger son, George.

George was twenty-one months younger than Joe and a constant companion. Their little sister, who was named Florence after their mother, was eleven years younger. As the baby of the family, she was pampered. Another brother, Franklin, had died in infancy. Angelo was a devoted Democrat, and the baby was named after Franklin Delano Roosevelt.

Joe's mother was a telephone operator and homemaker known for her Sunday dinners of heaping portions of manicotti and lasagna. She inspired her children to think big. Said Paterno in his 1989 autobiography, *Paterno: By the Book*, "Mom never took a back seat to any one, any place, any time. If she couldn't be at the head of the pack, she wouldn't go. So, as the first son, in anything I did, I had to be at the top."

Joe's love for football began on the streets of Flatbush. He played the game for hours with neighborhood kids, who used manhole covers and street curbs as boundaries. A Boy Scout and an altar boy, Joe may not have been the biggest or most talented kid in those pickup games, but he was the most intense. During one game he was so focused on catching a pass that he ran face-first into a tree and split open his lip. He would show the scar to anyone who cared to see it.

Even back then he believed he was destined to do great things. After graduating from St. Edmond's Grammar School, Joe and George enrolled in Brooklyn Preparatory High School, a prestigious private school in the Crown Heights neighborhood adjoining Flatbush. Their father worked second and third jobs to pay the tuition. Joe's self-determination was strengthened by the teachings of the Jesuit priests at Brooklyn Prep, and he and George were great assets to the school. Joe was the quarterback on their winning football team and the captain of their basketball team. He was also the senior class president. George also distinguished himself as a scholar and an athlete.

The school had a strict dress code, with students required to wear jackets and ties to class. The curriculum was comprehensive, with courses in calculus, Greek, and Latin. Joe loved to translate ancient stories from Latin to English just for the fun of it. One of his Jesuit instructors, Father Thomas Bermingham, taught him the story of Aeneas, the mythical hero who fled ancient Troy after the war to found the Roman Empire. Joe saw parallels between football and Virgil's epic poem, *The Aeneid*. His favorite part of the poem, which he related many times, was when Aeneas left the burning city of Troy carrying his father on his back and holding the hand of his son—a metaphor for preserving the past while nurturing the future. To Joe, Aeneas was the ultimate team man. His copy of *The Aeneid* was in Latin; he had translated the poem line by line, and it remained a favorite piece of literature long after he left Brooklyn Prep.

While he excelled in his studies, it was on the high school football team that Joe made a name for himself. He was a scrappy, left-handed quarterback, and his younger brother was a bruising fullback. The local newspapers took note of their play and named them "the Gold Dust Twins." In Joe's senior year Brooklyn Prep's football team was regarded as the best Catholic high school team in New York City. Still, it lost a playoff game to St. Cecilia High School of Englewood, New Jersey, coached by another future legend, Vince Lombardi. Lombardi, who also grew up in Flatbush, went on to coach the Green Bay Packers, which won five National Football League championships in seven years. Every year since 1967 Super Bowl victors are awarded the Vince Lombardi Trophy.

Joe also played baseball, but he wasn't very good. In fact, when his high school coach, Earl Graham, saw him swing a bat, he said, "You couldn't hit a bull's ass with a banjo." But baseball influenced Joe in another way. In 1943, when Joe was seventeen, Graham took him to see the New York Yankees play in the World Series. During the game the coach pointed out how polished the Yankees were, with shiny shoes and well-fitting pinstriped uniforms, unlike the scruffy uniforms of their opponents, the St. Louis Cardinals. When the Yankees won the title, Joe assumed the team's groomed appearance had contributed to their success. He liked the idea of conservative, simple uniforms worn with dignity and respect.

During his high school days Joe earned spending money by working as an usher at Ebbets Field in Flatbush, home of the Brooklyn Dodgers. In those days everyone sitting on the stoops or tenement steps in the summer had his radio tuned to the Dodgers game, with Fred "Dixie" Walker playing right field, Joe "Ducky" Medwick in left, Gil Hodges on first base, and Leo "the Lip" Durocher at shortstop.

Joe loved the pickup games at Marine Park on Jamaica Bay. On weekends all the kids from Flatbush rode their bikes there, to the Pratt-White Athletic Field, to play for hours. Even though Joe's sports were football and basketball, he was athletic enough to hold his own. He played with the older brothers of the famous New York Yankees' manager Joe Torre, who was a Flatbush native and thirteen years Joe's junior. Joe once dated Torre's sister, Marguerite. He was a bit of a celebrity himself because of his football exploits with Brooklyn Prep.

After receiving his high school diploma in 1945, Joe was drafted into the U.S. Army; he was stationed at Fort Dix, New Jersey. World War II was coming to an end, so he never saw combat overseas. He was sent to Korea, however, where the U.S. Army accepted the surrender of Japanese soldiers in the southern part of the country. He was granted an early discharge in 1946 to enroll at Brown University, courtesy of a benefactor named Everett "Busy" Arnold, who underwrote the cost of a college education for students who could play football. Arnold was a 1921 graduate of Brown University who had struck it rich in New York publishing comic books. He wanted his alma mater to be competitive against rival Ivy League schools such as Yale, Harvard, and Princeton. He had heard through the grapevine of the athletic achievements of the Paterno brothers from Flatbush and, in a practice that was legal at the time, paid the tuition for both brothers to attend Brown.

Despite Arnold's generosity, Joe was not immediately comfortable amid the snobbery at Brown. As a freshman he once attended a fraternity party dressed in a pair of slacks and a white sweater. Unfortunately everyone else was wearing blue blazers and navy striped ties. Joe overheard one of the rich Wasp students utter an ethnic slur offensive to Italians, "How did that dago get invited?" He was hurt by the comment but rose above it, determined to prove that he was just as smart as or smarter than those haughty New Englanders. In time he did become a member of a different fraternity, Delta Kappa Epsilon.

Even though he was just five-feet-eight and weighed 160 pounds, he stood out on the football field. In addition to playing quarterback, he finished his career with fourteen interceptions as a defensive back, setting a school record that has yet to be surpassed. In his last two seasons the Bears won fifteen games and lost only three. Joe won games out of sheer competitiveness more than athletic ability. Stanley Woodward, the sports editor of the *New York Herald Tribune*, wrote of Joe, "He can't run and he can't pass. All he can do is think and win."

JOE ARRIVED AT PENN STATE with some clothes, his vinyl records of Verdi and Puccini operas, and a few of his favorite books. He moved into a spare bedroom in Engle's new house, not far from campus. He had made a deal to board with his new boss for a year.

Penn State had 12,000 students and State College had 20,000 residents in 1950. The small town, conservative in its politics and religious views, had none of the hustle and bustle or sharp elbows of Brooklyn or Providence. There were two main streets, College Avenue, near the campus, and Beaver Avenue. Pennshire Clothes, Woodrings Floral Gardens, and the Warner Theater mixed with banks, drugs stores, the laundromat, a bookstore, and a dozen churches. Townies and students alike ate at The Diner on College Avenue, just a block from campus; the railway car diner had been there since 1929. The Tavern was the only restaurant that served anything close to Italian; spaghetti was on the menu, but there was celery in the sauce.

His mother's genuine homemade spaghetti sauce had lots of tasty spices, but not celery.

The football stadium, Beaver Field, was a down-at-the-heels facility built in 1909. It was only a couple of blocks from Engle's house. Penn State attracted an average of 21,000 fans for its four home games the year Paterno and Engle arrived.

Joe's first impression of provincial State College wasn't favorable. A couple of weeks in he told Engle to start looking for another assistant because being in a town that small and isolated was going to drive him nuts. But after the culture shock eased, he grew to love the place. There was something alluring about the open spaces and the forested ridges of the Appalachian Mountains. Penn State was a hard place to get to, but it was harder to leave.

As Engle's assistant coach, Joe was a loyal apprentice. In fact, he became the coach's eyes and ears. At Engle's urging, he moved into a dormitory where fifty members of the Nittany Lions football team occupied the first two floors. Joe served as the dorm monitor. If he heard of bad conduct, such as players drinking or skipping class, he reported it to his boss. Players secretly called him "Joe the Rat" for his snitching. He was "Joe the Rat" for his appearance too. At rainy games and practices, his thick black hair would fall down over his face and his big Italian nose poked out, giving him the appearance of a rodent. But Joe never worried about his popularity, just his effectiveness in getting the best out of his players. "You can't be a nice guy and do this job," he would say.

After several seasons at Penn State, Joe confided to his father that he intended to coach as a career and not pursue a law degree. "Whatever you do, make an impact," Angelo told his son. "Don't waste your life just winning football games. Have an impact." Joe gave his father his word. He had been at Penn State for five years when Angelo died, in September 1955. Joe went home to Flatbush to grieve with his family, which caused him to miss Penn State's game against Army. It was the first of only three games he would miss in his six decades of coaching. In honor of his mother and father, he would later establish a fellowship in the Department of Political Science, the Florence and Angelo Paterno Graduate Fellowship in the Liberal Arts.

In 1959 he met Suzanne Pohland, a perky first-year English literature major from the southwestern Pennsylvania town of Latrobe, home of Rolling Rock beer and the golfer Arnold Palmer, in the Penn State library. She was eighteen and he was thirty-one, and they shared a love of literature. They discussed the literary merits of *The Adventures of Huckleberry Finn* and Camus's *The Stranger*. Sue eventually fell in love with the scholar in him, and they were married soon after she graduated three years later. En route to Virginia Beach for their honeymoon, Sue learned just how much she would have to share her new husband when Joe stopped in Somerset County to pay a visit to a football recruit while she waited in the car. From the start it was clear that football was his life and she would have to accept that.

Sue taught English for one year at Bellefonte High School before she gave birth to a daughter, Diane, in 1963. Four more children—May Kay, David, Scott, and Joseph Jr.—would follow. To accommodate the family, Joe and Sue bought a modest stone-and-glass ranch house at 830 McKee Street in State College, where they lived for forty-nine years.

Paterno had the habit of wearing his best pair of wool slacks on game days, and invariably the cuffs would be spattered with mud as he paced the sidelines. Sue suggested that he roll up the cuffs to save on dry-cleaning bills. Because his dress shoes also took a beating on the muddy sidelines, he opted to wear sturdy black football shoes; they fit best when worn over thick white socks. Thus was born the Paterno look.

Paterno was tempted to leave Penn State in 1964, when Yale University offered him the job of head coach. The thought of running his own program at an Ivy League school appealed to him, but first he needed to know if he would be in line for the Penn State slot when Engle retired. Engle had endorsed Paterno as his heir apparent and even accompanied him to a meeting with the university's administration. No promises were made, but Paterno was told he would get the job if the school thought he was the best choice. As a result he turned down Yale's offer. When Engle did retire after the 1965 season, Paterno's patience paid off. He was awarded the head coach's job.

Joe had such a good relationship with Penn State by this time that the formality of a contract wasn't necessary. He agreed to take the position on a handshake for a salary of $20,000, a comfortable income at the time. At the age of thirty-eight, he launched an ambitious program to take Penn State football to a higher level. The Nittany Lions hadn't had a losing season in twenty-seven years, but their opponents were mostly from the eastern United States and were not considered as powerful as teams such as Alabama, Oklahoma, Texas, Notre Dame, and the University of Southern California. Penn State and its regional rivals competed for the Lambert Trophy, a sort of consolation prize. Joe wanted to win national championships against the best opponents out there, but he also wanted to win with scholar-athletes.

Paterno called his ambitious plan the Grand Experiment. To explain the plan, he asked the players he recruited, "What if we have the best of both worlds? What if Penn State kids were smart enough to graduate from Harvard and athletic enough to beat Alabama?"

CHAPTER TWO

———

THE AGE OF PATERNO

The Age of Paterno looked nothing like the Age of Aquarius, that rebellious time in the 1960s when a generation became enamored with the long-haired look made popular by the Beatles. Joe asserted his authority immediately upon becoming head coach. Penn State football players were not among those breaking from established traditions or openly questioning authority, like their contemporaries, the antiestablishment hippies. Their new coach insisted on honorable behavior. Appearance-wise, he set the standard for short hair and forbade beards and mustaches. Shirts had to have collars; wearing shoes without socks was unacceptable. Members of his inaugural recruiting class said that Paterno thought bare ankles in shoes was one of the worst looks in the world. When he took over as coach, it was traditional for male fans to wear blue blazers and neckties to games. Crowds were staid and stoic. It was considered in bad taste to cheer too loudly.

A trend at the time was to put the names of players on the backs of jerseys. Joe would have none of that. Aeneas would never put names on the backs of his soldiers' uniforms, he reasoned. He maintained the understated look of the Penn State uniform until very late in his career. In the coach's eyes, it was all about team, not individuality.

For Joe Paterno, football was a world unto itself. He even had groundskeepers paint a blue line around the football field to demarcate the boundaries of his empire. Once a player crossed that blue line, he was supposed to leave behind all distractions and give his complete attention to football. Outsiders weren't invited. Practice sessions were closed to the sports writers who covered the team. Those practices were pretty intense. Players said it wasn't uncommon for him to grab a guy by the facemask and look directly into his eyes as he was screaming at him. Practices were also filmed; a camera recorded everything that went on, ostensibly to see how players were performing, but Big Brother was watching all the time.

Joe spent hours alone in his office at home devising formations and game plans. He was so busy during football season his family would see him only at dinnertime; then he would go back upstairs to his office to strategize, usually while listening to his operas.

His game plans were conservative, and they were the same in his first victory as they were in his last: play strong defense, be sound in the kicking game, and don't turn the ball over to the other team with fumbles or interceptions. Charles Pittman, a running back who was a member of Joe's inaugural recruiting class, joked that Penn State played offense only because the rules dictated it.

When Pittman arrived on campus for his freshman year in 1966, 99 percent of the student body was white, and State College still had businesses that were segregated. Pittman and his roommate, the linebacker Jim Kates of Plainfield, New Jersey, were the only African Americans on the team.

The son of a steelworker from Baltimore's inner city, Pittman was a prized candidate for the Grand Experiment. He was the captain of the Edmonson High School football team, which never lost a game when he was there. Scoring more points than any other player in the state of Maryland helped land him a spot on *Parade Magazine's* High School All-American Team. He was also a scholar, voted most likely to succeed by his classmates.

Pittman entertained scholarship offers from Notre Dame, Ohio State, and Maryland, but he chose Penn State even though Rip Engle was leaving and Paterno was just taking the reins.

To Pittman, Paterno was more of a life coach than a football coach. Pittman recalled a time at the start of his first football camp, when freshmen were subjected to the ritual of singing the alma mater for the entertainment of the upper classmen. The older players were letting the new guys know that although they may have been superstars in high school, they were starting out on the bottom rung at Penn State. Pittman felt uncomfortable when it was his turn to sing, and Paterno sensed his awkwardness. He told the other team members, "Maybe we'll save that for a later day." It wasn't a pass; everybody on the team had to conform to the same rules, and Pittman did sing some days later, after he had adjusted to his surroundings. But he was impressed that Paterno was sensitive to his feelings. "He was a tough task-master," Pittman said. "He would yell and scream in that high-pitched Brooklyn accent of his and get into some guys' faces when he thought it was appropriate. But I never responded to yelling and screaming. He would put his arm on my shoulder and tell me to be the best player possible. He had a way with people. He was controlling, but all football coaches are controlling. I mean, we all voted to elect captains, but Joe was the one who counted the votes. He had eyes and ears everywhere. He knew everything that was going on."

Paterno's first game as a head coach was a 15–7 win over Maryland on September 17, 1966, in front of 37,270 fans at Beaver Stadium, which changed its name from Beaver Field in 1960. The rookie coach was awarded the game ball afterward. The sophomore defensive tackle Mike Reid scored the first points of the Paterno era by blocking a punt for a safety. Reid was also credited with two more safeties that day, accounting for six of his team's points. Although Reid had enrolled at Penn State under Engle, he was just the kind of player Paterno wanted for his Grand Experiment. A native of Altoona, Pennsylvania, Reid defied the stereotype that football players could lift pianos but not play them. He went on to win the Outland Trophy as the outstanding interior lineman in college football and after graduating became a concert pianist and a Grammy Award-winning musician.

Charles Pittman didn't crack the starting lineup until the fourth game of his sophomore season, and then only because of an injury to the running back Bobby Campbell. Penn State had lost seven of its first thirteen games under Paterno, but with Pittman as a starter the Nittany Lions beat Boston College by a score of 50–28 on October 14, 1967. Penn State didn't lose another game until after Pittman graduated in 1970.

The year before Pittman left, Penn State's offensive line coach Joe McMullen took a job in San Jose, California. Paterno filled his vacancy with two people, both former graduate assistants. One was Jim Weaver and the other was Jerry Sandusky. Weaver was in charge of the center and the guards. Sandusky was in charge of tackles and tight ends.

Paterno had known Sandusky as a player at Penn State and had hired him as a graduate assistant in 1966. Sandusky then left for a series of other coaching positions. Paterno brought him back in 1969 for the McMullen position. Then, when the defensive coach Dan Radakovich left Penn State to become the defensive coordinator at the University of Cincinnati, Paterno asked Sandusky if he would switch to defense. "I'll take it. I'll take it," Sandusky said. Before Radakovich left, he tutored Sandusky on the finer points of Penn State's defense, and Sandusky compiled a defensive scheme the size of a city phone book.

Sandusky was a little surprised when Paterno first invited him back. The two had never been friends, and when he was a graduate assistant for the team, Paterno had often criticized him for being a goofball. However, he thought enough of Sandusky's coaching ability to offer him the position.

CHAPTER THREE

SANDUSKY MAKES
HIS MARK

Jerry Sandusky returned to Penn State at the age of twenty-five. For two years he had been on what those in his profession call "the coaching carousel." He had served as a football assistant and basketball coach at Juniata College in Huntingdon, Pennsylvania, a liberal arts college of 1,100 students located just thirty miles south of Penn State. He uprooted again in 1968 to become the offensive line coach at Boston University, a big-city school with a football team on the competitive college level. Then came the call that changed his life. Joe Paterno offered him a chance to return to Penn State as an assistant coach.

Sandusky would be back on the campus with the tree-lined paths and columned buildings in the shadow of Mount Nittany. He set down roots after that eight-hour drive from Massachusetts and would never leave the area again.

Sandusky had first come to Penn State in the autumn of 1962 as a wide-eyed freshman looking to find his way in life. He had been offered scholarships by several colleges because of his talents as a football player.

He chose Penn State because he liked the pastoral setting, the football program was solid, and the school had a good academic reputation. One of his high school teammates, a running back named Bob Riggle, had also chosen Penn State, so Sandusky was going to know at least one other freshman player. He received a full scholarship to play football. In those days players played both offense and defense, but Sandusky was better suited to play defense. He wanted to get a degree in physical education, which might lead to a job as a teacher.

His father, Arthur, was a big sportsman long before he met his wife, Evelyn Mae "Evie" Lee. The two had grown up three doors apart from each other in the town of Washington, Pennsylvania, 150 miles west of State College. But it was sports that ultimately brought them together. A tomboy, Evie played in neighborhood baseball games with her six older brothers, and during one of those games she was on the opposing team against her future husband. They were married on July 25, 1942; their only son, Gerald Arthur, was born eighteen months later, on January 26, 1944.

Art was a trolley conductor and Evie was a housewife. To earn extra money, the couple opened a neighborhood business called Art's Ice Cream Stand. When Jerry was eight, Art was asked to take over as director of the local recreation center, the Brownson House, named for Judge James Brownson of Washington County. Judge Brownson had purchased the former corporate offices of the Tyler Tube and Pipe Company and turned it into a gymnasium and activity center for neighborhood kids. The Brownson House had operated for fifteen years before being closed for a time when juvenile vandals did so much damage to the brick-and-stone building that it didn't seem worth salvaging. Art quit his job at the trolley company to accept the director's job in 1952 for a salary of $100 a month and a rent-free apartment on the third floor.

At the Brownson House, Evie taught nursery school and led a Brownie troop. Art did the cleaning, painting, plumbing, and electrical work. He also cut the grass, took care of the ball fields, and dug ditches to keep the community center in good working order. As its director, he supervised sports activities such as football, basketball, baseball, softball, wrestling, boxing, and gymnastics. He coached a football team called the Brownson

House Bears, an amateur squad that grew out of the community center. A football field that adjoins the Brownson House is named after him. Art also played baseball in the minor league system of the St. Louis Cardinals for one year. He managed a youth baseball team in the PONY league, short for Protect Our Neighborhood Youth. His 1955 team won the PONY League World Series. He also started the Pennsylvania Junior Wrestling program, now known as Junior Olympics. For a lifetime of helping kids at the Brownson House, he was inducted into the Pennsylvania Sports Hall of Fame for "meritorious service" to youth.

Art was well respected in the community, especially for his work with underprivileged kids. He always exhibited exemplary behavior around children. The sign in his office said, "Don't give up on a bad boy, because he might turn out to be a great young man."

The Brownson House provided Jerry with all kinds of new playmates. He called the place "the Bug House" because he thought the zany regulars met the definition of "crazy" or "buggy." Like his parents, he found an outlet in sports. At Clark Elementary School he played midget football. His junior high school basketball team was undefeated. He was also on the football, baseball, and track teams at Washington High School. Besides sports, he was an elected member of the student council and and ran the film projectors for the Student Operators Society.

Jerry was also a prankster, according to several boyhood friends. One time in the high school chemistry lab he rubbed the earpiece of the telephone with charred cork, then snuck out and placed a call to the lab. When the teacher answered and put the phone to his ear, the charred cork left a black ring. Jerry and his friends liked to play tricks on the couples who parked along a lovers' lane in Washington Park. Jerry would borrow his father's red Ford pickup truck, equipped with a siren. With his buddies riding in the bed of the truck, Jerry would drive to the lovers' lane and turn on the siren, watching in amusement as the occupants of the cars scrambled to put their clothes back on. Those same friends said that Sandusky never dated in high school or went to the prom, but he did play football well enough to get a full scholarship to perform under Rip Engle at Penn State.

Evie and Art hoped Jerry's mischievous days were over when they drove their son to State College for his freshman year. One of the last legs of the trip took them by the yellow cornfields and rural villages along the winding curves of scenic State Route 45, a one-time stagecoach route that still shares the right-of-way with horse-drawn Amish buggies.

At Penn State Jerry was shy and didn't date or go to many college parties. When he did hang out with buddies, he pulled childish stunts, like throwing water balloons from car windows. He was most at ease on team sports. He won the first of his three varsity letters as a sophomore. During his first year the Nittany Lions won seven of the ten games they played. They never had a losing season when Jerry was on the team.

In the summer of his senior year he met his future wife at a picnic in Little Washington. Dorothy "Dottie" Gross, originally from Chattanooga, Tennessee, had lived in Little Washington for years but had never met Jerry Sandusky. Her family had recently moved to Chicago, so she was staying with friends in town for the summer. Jerry was a few months older than Dottie. She had red hair, worn in the bouffant style of the 1960s. At first Jerry couldn't work up the nerve to ask her out on a date. His mother encouraged Dottie to watch him play in a softball game, and after the game he drove her home. She'd stop by the playground where he was working as the director and even helped him organize games with the kids. One time Dottie and Jerry went with a group to see the Pittsburgh Pirates play at Forbes Field. After she went back to Chicago, they stayed in touch through letters. In one Jerry told her, "You are my destiny."

Jerry and Dottie were married in September 1966, three months after he graduated from Penn State with a degree from the College of Health Education. Number one in his class, he was the student marshal at the commencement ceremony.

AS PATERNO'S ASSISTANT, SANDUSKY COACHED the tackles on the offensive line. The chief guru of the defense was Assistant Coach Dan Radakovich, who had such success developing star players that he was called the Dean of Linebacker U. That year Penn State was undefeated for the second straight season, and the Nittany Lions were on their way to national prominence. When Radakovich left in 1970 to take a job at the University of Cincinnati, Sandusky assumed the responsibilities of coaching Penn State's linebackers.

All the while Jerry and Dottie were living in a small house near the university. They wanted to start a family, but sadly discovered they couldn't have children of their own. Jerry, however, did not lose faith. He was guided by a popular Sandusky family saying: "It's not what happens to you, but how you react to it." They served as fosters parents for several children through the child welfare agencies of Centre County and the Pennsylvania State Foster Parent Association. Then they decided to go the adoption route. Over the course of three decades they adopted three infants and three older foster kids, Kara, E.J., Jon, Jeff, Ray, and Matt. Kara, the oldest, was adopted after having been one of their foster children. Matt, the youngest, was taken in as a foster child at age sixteen and adopted two years later. The three adopted in infancy were found through appropriate agencies and adopted over twenty-eight years. Jerry's motivation behind caring for foster kids and adopting the infants came from the work his parents did helping kids at the Brownson House.

Eventually the Sanduskys moved to a five-bedroom, 3,000-square-foot house on Grandview Road, right off East College Avenue. Four of the Sandusky children—Kara, Ray, E.J., and Jon—graduated from Penn State. E.J. was the starting center for the 1992 Nittany Lions and later served as head football coach at Albright College and as assistant coach at West Chester University. Jon was a two-year letterman as a defensive back at Penn State. After graduating in 2000 with a 3.79 grade point average in kinesiology, he served as a scout for the Philadelphia Eagles of the National Football League and later became the director of player personnel for the Cleveland Browns.

Jerry was at Penn State for eight years when he was named the university's defensive coordinator, a position that made him a top lieutenant on Paterno's staff. That year he wrote and self-published a manual on his coaching specialty, *Developing Linebackers*. It became a teaching tool on how to play the position. He used the meager proceeds from the book to launch a charity for disadvantaged youth, The Second Mile. It was incorporated in 1977. With legal help provided by a Penn State professor, The Second Mile was granted tax-exempt status that same year.

In the beginning Jerry ran the charity from his house, mentoring troubled kids, involving them in games and athletic endeavors in hopes of helping them turn their lives around. By 1980 he had raised $64,000 from the sale of his book, which he used to buy twenty acres of farmland two miles from Beaver Stadium, just outside State College. He built and opened a group home on the property, to be occupied by six "at risk" boys from the State College area and run by hired house parents. Local businesses donated the supplies to build it, and a local contractor constructed it for the cost of his labor. The first six boys took residence in 1982. They had been chosen to live there by local social agencies.

Once the home was up and running, it was easier for Jerry to solicit donations. Eventually The Second Mile opened its headquarters in State College and had offices in Harrisburg and the Philadelphia area. The charity reached out to children in all sixty-seven of Pennsylvania's counties.

Besides running The Second Mile, Jerry served as the director of a summer football camp at Penn State that was sponsored by the university. The camp attracted hundreds of kids from all over Pennsylvania. Motivational speakers came to talk to the kids, and Joe Paterno sometimes made an appearance. Among the many volunteers was Guy Montecalvo, a native of Little Washington who had been mentored by Jerry's parents at the Brownson House. Montecalvo had played football at Washington High School and was recruited by Sandusky to play at Penn State on a scholarship. At the Penn State football camp he helped entertain the campers with music and comedy skits. As an amateur singer and a piano player, he joined Sandusky in forming an impromptu singing group called the Bobbin' Robins, which Jerry later changed to the Great Pretenders.

Montecalvo remembered Sandusky as a fun person. His interactions with the campers were of a playful nature. He was always in the middle of some activity, such as volleyball games or splashing around in the swimming pool. "The Jerry Sandusky I knew was a role model for what he did as a football coach and for the kids he reached out to at The Second Mile," Montecalvo said. "He seemed to be one of the most compassionate and altruistic individuals I ever met." Montecalvo insisted he never once saw any odd behavior involving Sandusky and a camper.

IN 1990 PRESIDENT GEORGE H. W. BUSH cited The Second Mile as the 294th example of his Thousand Points of Light. Suffice it to say The Second Mile garnered a lot of attention and support because of Sandusky's relationship with Penn State. There was no way the charity would have grown so expeditiously without the benefit of its relationship with a high-profile university. Bush considered Joe Paterno a friend after Paterno campaigned for him in the 1980 Pennsylvania Primary. Paterno had also given a seconding speech on Bush's behalf at the Republican National Convention in 1988 in New Orleans.

The Penn State connection also helped Sandusky's annual charity golf tournament, which he started in 1981, by donating the use of its Blue and White golf courses. Soon former Penn State players were participating and big-name pro football players were lending their names to the event. The annual tournament, a popular three-day fundraiser, had honorary chairmen such as the former Penn State and NFL players Lenny Moore and Kyle Brady.

At its peak The Second Mile had $9.5 million in assets and $3 million in annual revenue. Its honorary board of directors was filled with important names in sports. Some of its distinguished directors included the former NFL coach Dick Vermeil, the Philadelphia Eagles coach Andy Reid, NFL Hall of Famers Franco Harris and Jack Ham, former Penn Staters and NFL players John Cappelletti and Matt Millen, the former Penn State president Bryce Jordan, the golfer Arnold Palmer, and the actor Mark Wahlberg.

"Jerry was like a saint up here," said Gary Gray, a former Penn State linebacker who was coached by Sandusky. "He was like a big kid. He was always touchy-feely. But he never drank or smoked, and I never heard him utter a curse word. He was a role model for a lot of people."

What helped The Second Mile succeed was Penn State's own achievement on the football field, due in no small part to Jerry Sandusky. He was the defensive mastermind who helped make Joe Paterno's Grand Experiment an ultimate success. Sandusky devised defensive schemes that could stop opposing offenses, such as stacking a defense to stop a strong running attack, or zoning a defense to confuse a strong throwing quarterback.

Penn State's first national championship came following the 1982 season in the Sugar Bowl, when the Nittany Lions defeated Georgia 27–23. Sandusky's defense largely held in check Georgia's star running back, Herschel Walker. Then, following the 1986 season, the 100th season of football at Penn State, the Nittany Lions won all eleven games and were ranked second in the country. They were pitted against top-ranked Miami in the Sunkist Fiesta Bowl, the first time a corporate sponsor had paid to have its name attached to a college football game. Penn State was the underdog, but Sandusky's defense forced seven turnovers, including five interceptions of Miami's quarterback Vinny Testaverde. The final interception came on fourth down with eighteen seconds left in the game and Miami just yards away from the winning goal. The 14–10 win marked Sandusky's finest hour as a defensive coordinator. He told sports writers afterward, "I've always prided myself on being able to handle pressure, but on that fourth down, I couldn't even speak to make the defensive call. When it was over, I just walked over to the bench and sat down by myself and cried." Playing against the future Hall of Fame wide receiver Michael Irvin and the highly touted running back Alonzo Highsmith, Penn State gave up 445 yards but allowed only one touchdown.

Athlon Publications, publisher of *Athlon Sports* magazine, named Sandusky the 1986 Assistant Coach of the Year. During the award ceremony Sandusky said, "Penn State's my home. It's more than just a place to make a living. It's a place my family and I all love. Penn State spoils you. It's just a great place to raise a family. I don't know that you can explain the attraction. It's a lot of small things. I guess you have to experience it."

Working under Joe Paterno wasn't easy. He was the dominant male on the football staff; what he said was gospel, and his assistants served obediently. There was friction because Joe would sometimes make the calls on defense and offense, taking away the responsibilities from his defensive and offensive coordinators. As early as 1966, when Sandusky was still a graduate assistant, Paterno was angry with him for getting to a drill late. Paterno was persnickety and had everything timed to the minute. Sandusky made a gesture as Paterno yelled at him to get with the program. He hadn't noticed it at the time, but he saw it when he watched the films from the practice later. The next morning Paterno called Sandusky into his office and chewed him out. Sandusky mentioned the incident in *Touched: The Jerry Sandusky Story*, which he wrote the year after his retirement from Penn State. He recalled that Joe told him, "I would like to be able to recommend you for future coaching jobs, but I don't want to recommend a guy who's going to act like a complete goofball."

When Matt Paknis joined the coaching staff as a graduate assistant in 1987, he sensed some negative feelings about Sandusky, but nobody said anything publicly. He thought Sandusky was cordial enough, but there was something creepy about the way he always surrounded himself with kids from The Second Mile. Sandusky had kids from the charity with him at team functions, on the team bus, at the games at Beaver Stadium, everywhere he went. Paknis claimed that he was hypersensitive to men who enjoyed the company of minors, having been abused by a neighbor when he was a boy. He believed his radar was sensitive enough to pick up something no one else seemed to have noticed.

"He was the Pied Piper," Paknis recalled. "I remember kids being around him all the time. I never saw him do anything overt, but I always thought there was something weird about him. It was a boundary issue. He was always touching the kids. You cross the line when you touch kids. You don't put your hands on kids."

WITH SANDUSKY COACHING DEFENSE, Penn State continued to win on the football field. The Grand Experiment kept churning out victories as well as graduates, and by 1999 Sandusky was the senior assistant on Paterno's staff. His success was so well known that he was considered by everyone in the football program to be Paterno's heir.

For years there was speculation that Paterno was going to retire. He was seventy-eight-years old, far older than most active coaches. He was already a grandfather seventeen times. He often talked about retiring, fueling speculation about who would replace him. For a time a prime candidate was the offensive head coach Fran Ganter. Like Sandusky, Ganter had played for the Nittany Lions and had been on the coaching staff for many years. Tom Bradley's name was also often mentioned. He was younger than Sandusky and Ganter by a decade. He too was a former Nittany Lion and had been a full-time coach on Paterno's staff since 1980. But it was all a moot point because JoePa wouldn't leave.

In 1999 Jerry Sandusky appeared to be at the peak of his career. He was fifty-five, the perfect age to assume a head coach job somewhere else. That May Paterno informed him that he would never be offered the job of head coach at Penn State, regardless of when the position became available. Paterno's reason was that Sandusky's attention to his charity was taking too much time away from his duties as defensive coordinator.

On July 1 a news release was issued from the Sports Information Department announcing Sandusky's retirement. He had no plans to coach at another school; he was just ready to step down and call it a career. And he wanted to devote more time to The Second Mile. In a statement he said, "As the organization has grown, the demands for my hands-on involvement have increased dramatically. Then a retirement window opened up at the same time, and that made it more economically feasible to do something like this."

Sports writers scratched their heads at the way the announcement was made. After all, Sandusky had built quite a reputation as a defensive mastermind in his thirty-two years on the coaching staff. The Nittany Lions had won their only two national titles while he was the Dean of Linebacker U. Given Sandusky's credentials and length of service, those who covered the team figured there would be a big farewell news conference, with Joe Paterno in attendance to indulge Sandusky with glowing tributes. An announcement in a news release, even if it had been laudatory, seemed like an odd way to say goodbye.

As it turned out, there was no big farewell party. Paterno's reaction was confined to the news release: "We can't say enough about what he has brought to the football program as an exceptional coach, a fine player and a person of great character and integrity. The success that the Nittany Lions

have enjoyed over the last three decades is due in large part to the contribution of people on our coaching staff like Jerry Sandusky. Jerry always has
dreamed big dreams and, as he's proven with The Second Mile, he's someone who can turn hope into reality."

Penn State's athletic director Tim Curley was the one to release the
news of Sandusky's retirement. He too complimented Sandusky on his
career as a player and a coach. "His achievement as a human being is splen-
didly demonstrated by the thousands of youngsters he touches annually
through The Second Mile," he said in a statement.

Sandusky was eligible for a comfortable nest egg. At the age of fifty-five
his retirement package from the state retirement system qualified him for a
lump sum of $148,271 and a $58,898 yearly pension. As a tenured professor
of physical education, he was granted emeritus status at Penn State, which
allowed him to keep his rank and title. He would have unlimited access to
all football facilities and all recreational facilities. He could work out in the
weight room built for football players and shower in the team's locker room.
A parking pass for a campus lot was part of the package. Sandusky was
given an account under the university's computer system, and he was listed
in the faculty directory.

As another perk the university also provided him with an office in a
building across from the new Lasch Football Complex. Sandusky decorated the walls of his office with team photos, plaques, news clippings, and
a bronzed shoe; he had worn the shoe as a midget football player back at
Clark Elementary School. A number of awards for his work with troubled
youth were also on display. For example, in 1993 Sandusky and his father
had received the annual Human Rights Award presented by the Washington, Pennsylvania, Branch of the National Association for the Advancement
of Colored People. Sandusky had been presented with the Contribution to
Amateur Football Award in 1995 by the Philadelphia chapter of the National Football Foundation and College Football Hall of Fame. That same
year the YMCA had given him its Service-to-Youth Award. Just two weeks
before he retired Sandusky had been inducted into the Pennsylvania Sports
Hall of Fame, just as his father had been ten years earlier. By all appearances, he was a pillar of the community.

Sandusky stayed on as a consultant to the football team for the fall season of 1999. Before the final home game on November 14, the seniors on the team were introduced to the crowd. Among them was Sandusky's son Jon, a reserve defensive back. Sandusky himself was called onto the field to be recognized for his thirty-two years of service and his two championship rings. As he trotted out, he and Jon embraced at the fifty-yard line. An appreciative audience of 96,480 inside Beaver Stadium gave him a standing ovation. Afterward Sandusky said to the media, "I've been through so much with those [seniors] and to run out there with a son, I'm sure that's something every father would love the chance to do. . . . My memories of Penn State football will be of blue-collar, loyal people fighting their guts out."

Sandusky was named Assistant Coach of the Year by the American Football Coaches Association, and the Penn State Athletic Department set up a $5,000 scholarship in his name. About the occasion Joe Paterno said in a statement, "We're delighted to see Jerry honored in this fashion. Obviously, the awards committee recognized how uniquely qualified he was. Jerry is a man who has done honor to everyone in the coaching profession. He is a great football coach and even more outstanding human being."

Sandusky's final game on the sidelines was the Alamo Bowl against Texas A&M on December 28, 1999, in San Antonio. Derek Fox returned an interception thirty-four yards for Penn State's first touchdown, the only score the Nittany Lions would need. Sandusky's defense intercepted four passes and recovered a fumble in the 24–0 win. The Aggies were held to 80 net yards rushing and 122 passing. It was the only shutout victory in a bowl game under Paterno, and it was Penn State's first shutout win in a bowl since beating Alabama 7–0 in the 1959 Liberty Bowl. The defense was so good that entire season that two players, defensive lineman Courtney Brown and linebacker LaVar Arrington, were the first two selections in the NFL draft. At the end of the Alamo Bowl Sandusky was doused with Gatorade and carried to the middle of the field on the shoulders of his players. It was a triumphant finish to a successful career.

CHAPTER FOUR

———

THE FIRST CLUES

There were several unnerving events the year before Sandusky's sudden retirement from coaching. In May 1998 an angry mother contacted the campus police, who have jurisdiction over the buildings and grounds of Penn State University. She was distraught over what her eleven-year-old son had told her about his evening with Assistant Coach Jerry Sandusky. Her son's hair was wet when he got home, and when she asked him about it, he told her that he had showered with the coach in the Penn State locker room. She wanted Sandusky to be arrested.

The mother explained to the officer how her son had come to know Sandusky in the first place. The boy, an aspiring athlete, had been involved in The Second Mile for about four years. His first interaction with Sandusky was when he was seven, at a charity picnic at Spring Creek Park, a thirty-four-acre preserve about a mile from campus. The two had been in a skit together that day, and Sandusky had showed a genuine interest in the child. After that interaction Sandusky invited him to a Penn State football game, along with several other children from The Second Mile. The outing

included a tailgate party organized by Sandusky's wife. Over time a bond
of trust began to develop between the two. The child was being raised by a
single mother, who considered Sandusky a good father figure.

On the night the boy came home with wet hair, Sandusky had taken
him to the Penn State football complex. The mother told the officer the
coach had picked up her son at the house, but he did not tell her what they
would be doing that night. He had not mentioned a workout at Penn State
or anything about a shower. The mother had not been asked to provide the
child with a change of clothes, or even a towel.

When her son returned home, he told her that during the short drive
from the house to the campus, the coach had repeatedly rubbed his thigh
as he sat next to him in the passenger seat of his car, a silver Cadillac.
They parked at the Holuba Hall football building, where Sandusky promised him a private tour. They were the only ones in the building. Sandusky
handed the boy a pair of gym shorts, even though he was already wearing
gym attire. The two lifted weights for twenty minutes or so in the state-of-
the-art workout room, then went to the locker room. Sandusky started an
improvised game of "Polish bowling," the object of which was to roll a ball
of tape into a cup. The mother reported that the coach then started play-
wrestling with her son before persuading him to take a shower, even though
the boy was not perspiring.

She said the child had been so unnerved at the prospect of taking a
shower with a naked man that he chose a shower as far from Sandusky
as he could get. But Sandusky lured him over, saying he had a shower all
warmed up right next to him. As the boy cautiously approached, the naked
Sandusky grabbed him around the waist from behind and told him, "I'm
going to squeeze your guts out." He proceeded to bear-hug the child from
behind, holding the boy's back to his chest. He then lathered the child's
back with soap, took him into his arms, and lifted the boy up to the show-
erhead for a rinse.

According to the mother, her son was finally able to extricate himself
from the coach's grasp, dressed as quickly as he could, and asked Sandusky
to take him home. When she saw her son's wet hair and heard his story, she
contacted the campus police to report the incident.

Her account landed on the desk of Detective Ronald Schreffler, one of the forty-six members of the campus police force. The short, squat Schreffler was among the best investigators the department had. But his normal caseload was geared more to minor crimes involving the population of 44,000 students than to crimes involving children. He had jurisdiction over crimes and complaints that happened on campus and within five hundred yards of its perimeter. Most calls to the station were about drinking, drugs, or assaults of varying degrees. Calls regarding The Second Mile were limited to providing security for the kids who came to Penn State to attend the organization's summer camps or other events. The campus cops were always willing to help Sandusky and his charity whenever they could. Just about everybody in Happy Valley knew Sandusky or had heard of him. Because he had been building The Second Mile charity for more than twenty years, his reputation went beyond the football arena.

From the start, the mother's complaint against Sandusky was handled with extreme care. Schreffler wasn't doubting her or her son, but these allegations were against a man who was an icon in the community. He also wasn't the only person in authority looking into the complaint; by law the Centre County Department of Children and Youth Services, the area's child welfare agency, also had to be called in. Since it held a contract with The Second Mile for counseling services, the Centre County entity declared a conflict of interest and deferred the case to the Pennsylvania Department of Public Welfare in Harrisburg. The state-run agency assigned its own investigator, Jerry Lauro. Under Pennsylvania law the state is allowed sixty days to consider a complaint before it renders a decision or refers it for prosecution. Lauro's mandate was to gather facts, regardless of the implications the complaint might have at Penn State.

Initially Schreffler and Lauro listened to the mother's story and interviewed her son. Both investigators were concerned enough with what they heard to proceed. The possibility that Sandusky had showered with an eleven-year-old was extremely disturbing.

The mother's account was powerful, but the son's description of what happened was not enough to prove that Sandusky had committed a crime. The investigators weren't confident they could take the case very far because the child was reluctant to speak out against a man he revered as a role model. From the child's account, it was unclear whether Sandusky's acts were sexual or simply inappropriate behavior by a man who considered himself an overgrown kid. If the welfare official determined that the complaint was legitimate, he would be required to place Sandusky's name on the state's watch list for sexual predators, and his work with The Second Mile would come to an abrupt end.

The next step was to bring in a mental health professional to conduct a preliminary evaluation of the child to determine whether the scenario with Sandusky had the markings of a predatory pedophile. After a short examination, the State College-based expert determined the actions were not predatory. Still, the investigators didn't feel they had enough information; basically it was one child's vague words against a prominent man. So they asked the mother to invite Sandusky to her home to be surreptitiously monitored. Schreffler proposed to hide in a nearby closet to listen to the conversation. But Lauro declined to accompany him. The Penn State detective then enlisted Ralph Ralston, a detective with the State College Police Department, to assist him. Both detectives were in hiding when Sandusky arrived at the condominium on May 13, 1998.

The boy's mother got right to the point. She demanded to know why the coach had showered with her son and why he had given him a naked bear hug. More important, she wanted to know whether he was stimulated sexually by the encounter.

Sandusky was taken aback and answered the question evasively. Yes, he sheepishly admitted, he had showered with her son, but that was nothing new for him because he had showered with other boys from The Second Mile under his care. He also claimed the episode had not been sexual in nature. The mother then pressed him on whether their private parts had touched during the bear hug. Sandusky said that he wasn't sure. "I don't think so . . . maybe," he admitted in the conversation. The mother demanded that the coach never shower with another boy again, including her son, but Sandusky made no promises.

The encounter between the mother and Sandusky provided admissions from Sandusky, but the detectives needed more evidence to build a case of

molestation, especially since the mental health professional's report suggested that Sandusky did not fit the profile of a child molester. A second
confrontation with the coach was set up for six days later, but this time
Lauro, the state welfare investigator, was not made aware of it.

During the second meeting at the condominium, the boy's mother
posed her questions in stronger terms. She demanded that Sandusky never
have contact with her son again, and he agreed. His parting words to her
were "I understand. I was wrong. I wish I could get forgiveness. I know I
won't get it from you. I wish I were dead."

Although Lauro was unaware that a second meeting between Sandusky
and the child's mother had taken place, he agreed with Schreffler that it
was time to confront the coach directly. Rather than setting up an appoint-
ment that would give Sandusky time to prepare, the men wanted to conduct
a surprise interview. After two days of failed attempts to find him, on June
1, 1998, Lauro and Schreffler located Sandusky. They found him working
out in a Penn State football weight room. Lauro did all the talking. He
confronted Sandusky with the mother's complaint. After some prodding,
Sandusky admitted to showering with the boy, but insisted there was no
sexual intent. From his facial expression it was unclear whether Sandusky
was concerned about the accusations; he looked at the investigator inquisi-
tively, as if he were trying to fathom why anyone would accuse him of
harming a boy he cared so much about. Sandusky said he probably should
not have showered with the boy and promised not to do it again. As the
conversation ended, Sandusky repeatedly insisted he had done no wrong.
"It wasn't sexual, honest," he said. Sandusky did not seek legal counsel after
the contact with the investigators.

Lauro believed the probe merited more investigation. But just a few
days after the discussion with Sandusky, he learned from Schreffler that
Penn State police had closed the investigation and would not file charges.
Schreffler did not tell him who made the decision to end the investigation
or offer a clear explanation why.

Not until 2011 did the welfare investigator realize that he did not know
everything about what had transpired back in 1998. Lauro had not been
informed about the second meeting between Sandusky and the mother. He

had also not been given an opportunity to review the police report, which
he learned was ninety-five pages long. Had he known about Sandusky's
comments during that second meeting, the state's probe would likely have
taken a different course. In fact, when Lauro returned to Harrisburg after
his initial meeting with Sandusky, he told his superiors that he felt the
Penn State campus police wanted him out of the probe and out of town
as soon as possible. With little information to go on other than Sandusky's
denials, he too closed his case with an "unfounded" ruling, meaning the
welfare probe was dead as well. In 1998 he memorialized the event in a
one-page report.

Schreffler's file included narratives from the mother and son and the
mental health professional, but did not include any evidence that anyone
else had seen the incident. Also included in the report were three different statements from Sandusky, which were remarkably consistent. Support
personnel at the football workout facility had also been questioned; all said
they had seen nothing. But the detective had not questioned Joe Paterno or
anyone else in the football administration.

While Schreffler believed that Sandusky could be charged with a variety of molestation-related crimes, even if misdemeanor counts were pursued, he learned that the Centre County district attorney felt otherwise.
Prosecutor Ray Gricar told the officer that the he-said-she-said evidence
was laced with reasonable doubt. The child was skittish, the mother's statements were secondhand, there was no independent corroboration of anything, and a mental health expert had said the evidence didn't reveal the
markings of a sexual predator. And there were no prospects that any additional evidence would emerge. While Schreffler and the mother believed
the smoking gun was Sandusky's admissions, Gricar determined that those
admissions could become a plausible defense. If he charged Sandusky with
a crime, the well-regarded coach, who had readily admitted to showering
with other young men, could easily build a defense around the reasonable
doubt that there was anything sexual about the event. And that is just what
Sandusky said during the covert conversation with the eleven-year-old's
mother and when the investigators confronted him. Sandusky was as consistent in his commentary as he was vehement that while such an incident

may not be normal in the eyes of many, it was not a molestation or assaultive in any way. Schreffler's report was never turned over to the prosecutor's office.

Schreffler's bosses accepted Gricar's decision without ever talking with Gricar about it. Throughout the probe Schreffler reported his findings to Thomas Harmon, head of the Penn State Campus Police Department at the time.

Harmon, in turn, had at least four conversations about Sandusky with Gary Schultz, the Penn State administrator who oversaw the campus police department. Schultz was the one who alerted the university's general counsel, Wendell Courtney.

The president of Penn State, Graham B. Spanier, said he was never informed about the investigation. Neither was Joe Paterno, who stated later that no one from the campus police department had ever questioned him about Sandusky or the 1998 allegations of sexual misconduct.

Gary Schultz claimed that he had tried to keep information about the investigation quiet. Because it had been determined that Sandusky's actions did not rise to the level of criminality or even abuse, there was no reason to besmirch his name. In Happy Valley embarrassing secrets were kept under wraps at all cost, no matter whose welfare might be jeopardized by this code of silence. But in this matter, despite Schultz's efforts to keep the probe discreet, rumors about the incident were still bandied about. Cops are notorious gossips, and soon versions of the story of Sandusky and the boy in the shower were making their way through area police departments, local gin mills, and even in the halls of the Centre County Courthouse in Bellefonte.

SCHREFFLER WASN'T SATISFIED WITH SANDUSKY'S contrition, but he would keep those feelings to himself for years. It turned out Gricar made his decision without consulting anyone, not even Karen Arnold, the lawyer in his office who prosecuted child abuse cases. Much later, some would suggest Gricar had discussed the matter with others in his office. Gricar informed Schreffler of his decision just two days after Schreffler and Lauro confronted Sandusky in the weight room. Schreffler relayed the prosecutor's decision to Thomas Harmon or Harmon's boss, Gary Schultz. Neither of them sought an explanation from Gricar, or ever received one from him.

Gricar's explanation for not bringing charges against Sandusky will never be known. He was last seen on April 15, 2005, when he took a day off from work and left his hometown of Bellefonte. He called his girlfriend to say he was going for a drive. Twelve hours later she reported him missing. The following day Gricar's BMW Mini Cooper was discovered in the parking lot of the Street of Shops antique market in Lewisburg, Pennsylvania, about fifty miles east of Bellefonte. Gricar had been known to frequent the market in the past. Police found no evidence of foul play in the car, which was locked. They did take note of a cigarette smell and found ashes on the passenger side, which was remarkable because Gricar didn't smoke and prohibited smoking in his car. Search dogs couldn't find a scent, and an extensive search of the Susquehanna River produced no body.

Investigators looked into three possible scenarios: Gricar wanted to disappear; it was a homicide; or he had killed himself. Six months after the district attorney went missing, his laptop computer was found in the Susquehanna River two hundred yards downstream from the Lewisburg Bridge. The computer's hard drive was also recovered in the river shortly thereafter, but it was so badly damaged it yielded no information.

At the time of Gricar's disappearance he had just announced a successful high-stakes heroin investigation and the arrest of nine suspects on charges of heroin and cocaine trafficking. Among those arrested was the alleged leader of the New York-based ring, Taji Lee. Pennsylvania Attorney General Tom Corbett called it the "largest heroin operation ever seen in Centre County." At a press conference two weeks before Gricar disappeared, Corbett had praised the arrests, the officers who had participated in the sting, and Gricar in particular for his devotion to the undercover investigation.

In July 2011 Gricar's daughter, Lara, successfully petitioned a Centre County judge to have her father declared legally dead. Penn State officials had never asked him why he dropped the Sandusky case, and there was no record of an investigation having been launched in his office.

The mother of Sandusky's eleven-year-old accuser claimed she never got a satisfactory explanation of why the assistant coach hadn't been charged. State welfare officials said she had in fact accepted a brief explanation of the decision.

Four years later Sandusky was still showering with boys in the Penn State locker room. Even though he had been retired for several years, he was on campus using the facilities, within his rights.

CHAPTER FIVE

INDEPENDENT
ALLEGATIONS

Mike McQueary always dreamed of becoming a football coach at Penn State. For two years he had served as a graduate assistant on Joe Paterno's staff. After one more year in that position he hoped to get a less menial, full-time job as a coach at his alma mater. At twenty-seven, he was smart and athletic; he had been a quarterback for Paterno during his undergraduate years. With bright red hair and a hulking six-foot-three frame, he had come to Penn State after a notable high school career with the Little Lions at State College High School. He was a good enough player to have been recruited by a number of schools, but he decided to stay home and play for the coaches he had known since he was a kid. McQueary waited his turn to start behind players destined for professional stardom. He didn't earn the full-time starting quarterback job until 1997, when he was a senior. Once given the opportunity, he led Penn State to a 9–3 record and a place in the Citrus Bowl in Florida. His name still remains in the university's record book for most passing yards and total offense in a single game in his first start, against the University of Pittsburgh.

He also was a finalist for the Johnny Unitas Golden Arm Award, presented annually to the nation's most deserving senior quarterback.

After graduating he tried to earn positions on professional teams, the Oakland Raiders in California for one, and NFL Europe's team in Scotland. When he was unsuccessful, he worked as an assistant payroll clerk at Penn State for a year while he tried to wrangle a job on Paterno's coaching staff. He eagerly accepted a graduate assistantship when it was offered to him three years after he graduated.

In March 2002 almost everyone at Penn State had left campus for spring break. But Mike was staying put, enjoying the quiet. Watching a football movie on television, he was inspired to drive to Penn State football headquarters, where he wanted to pick up some tapes of prospective recruits to review. When he arrived just after 9 P.M., the complex was dark.

After he entered the dark halls of the Lasch Building, McQueary went first to the support staff locker room to drop off a new pair of sneakers. He walked past coaches' offices, an academic research center, workout facilities, rooms with whirlpools and saunas, and other fitness rooms in the state-of-the-art facility. As he was walking through the swinging wooden doors of the locker room, he heard a clap-clap-clapping sound that made him somewhat embarrassed; the sound seemed to be from wet skin-on-skin sex. His first thought was that one of the players had snuck into the complex with a paramour for some kinky action. Or maybe a custodian had brought someone in. McQueary moved gingerly toward the shower room and through the first set of double doors. As he opened the second set of doors, he looked over his shoulder at a mirror set at an angle that reflected directly into the shower room. There was the retired Penn State defensive coordinator Jerry Sandusky, naked with a prepubescent Caucasian boy who appeared to be no more than ten years old. The child was so small that Sandusky's body nearly enveloped him, the coach's hands wrapped around the naked child's waist. The embrace appeared to be sexual in nature.

"Jerry was directly behind him in a very, very, very close position, with Jerry's hands wrapped around his waist or midsection," McQueary recalled later in sworn testimony. He said his position just outside the shower room prevented Sandusky and the child from knowing he was there. He moved closer for a better look. Walking through the second set of doors, he saw that the child was facing the wall with his hands up against it. Although exactly what was going on was hidden, McQueary said it was clear to him that they were in a sexual position. "I believed Jerry was sexually molesting him and having some type of intercourse with him," he said. He testified that he did not see Sandusky's genitalia or penetration, but "that's what I believe was happening." Shocked and disturbed, McQueary retreated to the locker room and slammed his locker door shut to try to get Sandusky's attention. He then walked back into the shower room and saw that the man and the child had separated. Less than a minute had passed since he had first stumbled on the scene.

The three of them exchanged uncomfortable eye contact, but no words. "To be frank, I can't describe what I was feeling or thinking," McQueary said under oath. "Shocked and horrified, quite frankly, not thinking straight. I was distraught." He was stunned to see a man who was not only his former coach at Penn State, but also the father of two high school friends and college teammates, sexually abusing a child.

McQueary had always revered Sandusky, whom he had known since he was a young child, through sports and other activities. He considered the coach a down-to-earth, self-effacing gentleman always quick with a quip and a smile. McQueary had never given Sandusky's touchy-feely interactions with kids a second thought, because he knew of his work helping troubled children through The Second Mile, founded when McQueary was just two years old. Now, for a few seconds, he stared down the two as they stood wet and naked in the shower. McQueary wasn't able to say if the naked coach was sexually aroused because he didn't look at his private parts, only stared into his eyes. He said he was in such a state of shock that instead of saying anything or immediately taking the child away, he quickly exited the shower room.

Later he'd say he thought the child was safe because whatever had been happening had ended. Though the campus police headquarters was only a short distance from the Lasch Building, he didn't go there either. Instead he went directly to his second-floor office and called his father, John McQueary, manager of medical offices in the region, and a person he trusted to guide him. The elder McQueary asked his son to come home immediately. There he and his father had an hour-long discussion, joined halfway through by his father's friend and colleague, Dr. Jonathan Dranov. The three decided the younger McQueary should report the incident to Joe Paterno as soon as possible. McQueary went home to bed, then called the legendary football coach at about 8 o'clock the next morning, a Saturday.

"Coach, I need to come to your house and talk to you about something," McQueary said he told Paterno. "He said, 'I don't have a [full time coaching] job for you, so if that's what it's about, don't bother coming over.'" When McQueary told him it was much more serious than that, the coach told him to come over right away. There he and Paterno sat at the kitchen table, and he explained the reason for his visit.

"I saw Jerry with a young boy in the shower and it was way over the lines, extremely sexual in nature and I thought I needed to tell him about it," McQueary remembered years later. Out of respect for Paterno, he did not reveal the details of what he saw, but said he was sure the legendary coach got the picture. McQueary said Paterno, then seventy-eight years old, slumped back in his chair. The coach told him he was sorry he had to witness such a thing and pledged to take action. "He said, 'You've done the right thing. I know it is probably tough for you to come here and tell me this, but you've done the absolutely right thing,'" McQueary testified. Paterno told him others at the university would be in contact with him soon.

Despite the urgency projected by Paterno during that early morning meeting, nine days passed before McQueary was contacted by Athletic Director Tim Curley, a 1976 graduate of the university. Curley, a charismatic and influential man who put Penn State on the map in many sports beyond football, summoned him to a meeting with himself and Penn State Vice President Gary Schultz. Schultz had been in charge of the Penn State Campus Police back in 1998, when Sandusky's behavior with an eleven-year-old boy was called into question, so this would be the second time he was hearing about allegations of Sandusky's improper conduct with a minor.

Curley, Shultz, and McQueary met in a conference room at the Bryce Jordan Center, the school's basketball arena and home to the athletic director's office. "I told them I saw Jerry Sandusky in the showers with a young boy in what seemed was extremely sexual, over the lines and it was wrong," McQueary said later to a grand jury and in criminal court. He said he told the officials more than he told Paterno, but he again refrained from describing all of the lurid details. He later insisted, "I would have described them as extremely sexual and that some sort of intercourse was going on." He said he believed Curley and Schultz "thought it was serious what I was saying, that they would investigate it or look into it closely and they would follow up." Asked specifically if he told the officials that Sandusky was committing a sexual act against the child, he answered, "There is no doubt at all."

Sometime over the next two weeks Curley and Schultz paid an impromptu visit to President Graham Spanier. Without naming McQueary, they let him know about a football staff member's concern that Sandusky was behaving inappropriately with a child in the locker room showers. The meeting was very brief, and the two administrators provided a sanitized version of what McQueary says he had told them. Instead of an accusation of rape, they told Spanier the incident had involved "horsing around" or "horseplay" between Sandusky and the child. From their description, Spanier didn't think the incident was very serious.

Although they didn't provide the details that McQueary said he had given them, they did tell the university president they were not comfortable with Sandusky and The Second Mile kids using Penn State facilities anymore. Spanier approved their plan to instruct Sandusky to stop bringing children to the football facilities or programs. The former coach was also going to be told to surrender his keys to the football complex facilities, and Curley was going to let Sandusky know of his decision to report the incident to top officials of The Second Mile.

After their meeting Curley relayed the plans that would resolve the Sandusky issue to McQueary, who accepted what he was told with an "okay." McQueary never had another discussion with Schultz.

To fulfill his obligations to the president, Curley summoned Sandusky to a meeting. Initially the former coach did not admit he had even been at the Lasch Building on the night in question. At another meeting almost two weeks later he acknowledged being there for a workout without mentioning being caught naked by McQueary with a young child in the shower. Later Curley, who has no law enforcement experience, acknowledged the sanctions he issued against Sandusky were virtually unenforceable because the retired coach enjoyed emeritus status as a university retiree, on which he had negotiated lifetime use of the football facilities.

Curley later testified that he had met with John Raykovitz, the long-time head of The Second Mile and a child psychologist. Even though Curley did not believe Sandusky's actions in the shower rose to criminal conduct, he said he reported Sandusky to the charity because of McQueary's report. He described Sandusky's behavior as "inappropriate" and added, "I figured [the child] was probably a Second Mile person."

It remains unclear whether Raykovitz ever discussed the matter with Sandusky, but some Second Mile board members would later complain that they were never notified about Mike McQueary's allegations, or that Sandusky had been barred from bringing Second Mile children to the Penn State football facilities. The former coach was Raykovitz's close friend.

Gary Schultz also minimized McQueary's allegations. "I had the feeling there was some kind of wrestling around activity and maybe Jerry might have grabbed the young boy's genitals," he told a grand jury. Schultz admitted that any such conduct was clearly inappropriate but said, "The allegations came across as not that serious." As for criminality, Schultz said there was no indication of a crime. He didn't make any other reports. Yet he later said that he was under the impression that other Penn State officials—he did not say who—contacted a social service agency about the allegations. When Schultz learned that no one from Penn State had reported McQueary's allegations about the incident to an outside police or child welfare agency, the man charged with oversight of Penn State's police department said only, "Wow, I thought it was turned over."

He later admitted to the grand jury that when he heard McQueary's report, he knew about the 1998 allegation from the young mother who had wanted Sandusky arrested for his behavior with her son. Schultz would say much later that he didn't make a big deal out of the earlier report because he did not think it was right to impugn the reputation of a guy like San-dusky over child molestation accusations that did not merit prosecution.

In the 1998 case Schultz was aware that the Pennsylvania Department of Public Welfare was involved in the investigation. He also knew his own police department had collected almost a hundred pages of evidence and admissions from Sandusky in the earlier probe. He never read the reports, but figured if a prosecutor didn't believe they merited prosecution, the case was closed.

Schultz rationalized his not reporting Sandusky to authorities in 2002 or requesting an investigation into McQueary's report because he knew Sandusky personally. He believed the former coach may have been misunderstood. He said the man had always been a physical person. He always touched folks, young and old, during conversations. He frequently put friends in headlocks, slapped them on the back, grabbed arms and other body parts in physical displays of affection.

At the time, that was it. There was not even a cursory investigation by any police agency into McQueary's eyewitness account. The Penn State officials did not make any reports because they did not believe Sandusky's conduct was criminal. They made no effort to learn the identity of the ten-year-old child or get his version of what happened.

While the noninvestigation into Sandusky's actions in 2002 ended without internal or external reports being written, McQueary said neither Schultz nor Curley ever told him to keep the situation quiet. McQueary, as well as members of the football team and staff, said the only time they saw Sandusky with children on Penn State premises after that was during group activities at The Second Mile summer camps. However, they said the retired coach continued to use Penn State's weight room and other facilities. Sandusky did not surrender his keys to the facilities either.

McQueary himself never pushed the investigation further. In his mind, by talking to Schultz he had gone to the police. Within a year of his report McQueary was hired as a full-time assistant football coach. The rumors of Sandusky's interest in young boys was locker room fodder among football players who jokingly warned teammates to be careful not to "drop the soap in the shower" when Sandusky was around.

Despite his claims, McQueary continued to participate in Second Mile charity events. He played in a flag football game coached by Sandusky, as

well as a golf outing and other events for The Second Mile. He also saw
Sandusky in the football facilities on a weekly basis, albeit without children.

McQueary's father said he too talked with Schultz about the situation
during an unrelated business meeting shortly after his son's report. He told
Schultz, "There should be something done about it." The elder McQueary
said Schultz told him it was not the first time he'd heard allegations of
abuse at the hands of Sandusky, so John McQueary was under the impression that something substantial was going to be done.

Meanwhile Mike McQueary never made public his opinions about the
way university officials handled his report. He told a grand jury that his
last contact with Penn State officials about the incident occurred three
months after the shower scene. That's when Paterno asked him if he was
satisfied with the outcome. McQueary said he told the coach that he was
fine with it.

Eight years would pass before a state trooper trolling the Internet for
background information about Sandusky would run across a blog suggesting a former Penn State football graduate assistant now employed as a coach
saw Sandusky molesting a young boy in a shower. The investigator quickly
determined it was McQueary. At that point, investigators started focusing
on the incident in the shower. They sought to find out who on the Penn
State staff knew about it, what they knew and when they knew it. One of
the first people they went to for answers was Joe Paterno.

CHAPTER SIX

PATERNO'S IMPACT

Joe Paterno was a man who cared deeply about everybody in his circle. When Mike McQueary came to him with his upsetting account of what he had witnessed in the locker room, Paterno did what he thought was his obligation. He believed the best thing was to pass the problem to his own bosses, Tim Curley and Gary Schultz, who he felt were better equipped to deal with the situation legally and objectively. Once he reported to them and made sure McQueary was okay with the resolution the two men came up with, he returned to being the best coach and leader that he could.

Paterno was proud to be accessible to the State College community. His telephone number was listed in the phone book; he never moved to a fancy neighborhood. He wasn't ostentatious or technocratic. He never owned a cell phone or a computer or ever understood the social networks. But this one-time kid from Brooklyn had done great things by surrounding himself with great people.

Steve Smear was among his most ardent admirers. He was the co-captain of the undefeated Penn State teams in 1968 and 1969 and a member of Paterno's first recruiting class in 1966. Smear recently talked about what it was like to play for Joe: "He let us be students. He had guys who belonged in college. We were able to have a complete college experience."

Paterno's singular voice, demanding discipline from his players on the field, was impressed in Smear's memory. "That voice! We used to joke that we had to learn another language when he would scream in that Brooklyn accent," he said with a chuckle. "He had a voice that could cut through steel. But he'd also encourage you. A lot of times his bark was worse than his bite. We were fortunate to have a coach like him."

Paterno was also a stickler for being on time and remaining disciplined. "If you were late for a practice or a meeting, he would tell you that you let down one hundred teammates and the coaching staff. It was a fate worse than death. He would yell and scream and make you run laps. Sometimes I still have this dream that I'm late for a meeting, and I can still hear his voice in my head. I'm never late for anything because of him."

Smear said that he and his teammates called Joe's "clock" Paterno Time. "If he said be there at a certain hour, you had to be ten to fifteen minutes early. Joe had a saying, that if you keep hustling, something good will happen. If you watch his teams, they always keep hustling until the end.

"We were part of his family. He was legitimately interested in us as people. He was a unique guy. I have the utmost respect for him."

Charles Pittman was another JoePa devotee. The Nittany Lions' storied running back had reached a crossroads in his life in 1972. Until then football had defined him. In the thirty games in which he had been a starting player, the team had never lost a game. The only blemish was a 17–17 tie with Florida State in the 1967 Gator Bowl. Pittman was the first player to achieve All-American honors on the football field under Paterno, and he so excelled in the classroom he earned honors as an Academic All-American as well.

After graduating from Penn State, Pittman tried his hand at professional football, playing one season each with the St. Louis Cardinals and his hometown Baltimore Colts. In those two seasons he carried the ball only four times for seven yards. He was seriously considering continuing his career in the Canadian Football League when he met with Paterno on a return trip to State College. Once again Pittman got some fatherly advice. "Joe put his hand on my shoulder and told me I was trying to prove that my college career wasn't a fluke," Pittman said in an interview in December 2011. "He told me I didn't have anything to prove to anybody and that I should get on with my life. So I got on with my life."

With Paterno's help, Pittman got a job as an executive with Marine Bank in Erie, Pennsylvania, where he and his wife, Maurese, settled down and began raising a family. That job didn't work out, so he decided to pursue a career in the newspaper industry. He was hired as promotions manager for the Times Publishing Company of Erie, headed by Ed Mead, whose family had been newspaper publishers in northwestern Pennsylvania for a long time.

As the years passed, his son, Tony, built his own reputation as a star running back at Erie McDowell High School. Tony wanted to follow in his father's footsteps and play at Penn State, but he was considered too small to play major college football. To get another year of growth and extra training prior to college-level sports, he enrolled at Phillips Academy in Andover, Massachusetts, in his senior year. George H. W. Bush had gone to Phillips Academy, and he tried to talk Tony into attending Yale University, his alma mater. An offer from Yale followed, but Tony had his heart set on Penn State. Twenty-five years after his father scored his last touchdown for the Nittany Lions, Tony became a member of the 1990 recruiting class. "I trusted Joe with my son," Charles Pittman said. "There's not a parent who wouldn't want his son to play at Penn State. Foremost, Joe is an educator and builder of men."

Tony wore number 24, his father's number. He started at offense but soon switched to defensive back under Defensive Coordinator Jerry Sandusky. Tony wasn't a starter right away, but in the spring of 1993 he earned the Jim O'Hora Award, presented annually to the defensive player who has displayed exemplary conduct and attitude. The award is named for a former Penn State assistant coach who served on the coaching staff for thirty-one years. Tony's best season came in 1994, his senior year, when at cornerback he led the Lions with five interceptions. That season the team won all

twelve of their regular season games, as well as the Rose Bowl, claiming the
Big Ten Conference championship. When Tony was in the starting lineup,
the Nittany Lions won sixteen games and lost none. Like his father, he was
an Academic All-American. He earned a business degree and a master's
degree in business administration, and like his father, he became a successful business executive. As of this writing, he serves as a director in the
global supply chain services of Hewlett Packard.

The Pittmans were the first two-generation father-son combination to
play for Joe Paterno, but not the last. In the forty-six years that Paterno was
Penn State's head coach, twenty-six such combinations played for him. In
games that Charles and Tony Pittman started for Penn State, the Nittany
Lions were 45-0-1.

A year after his son graduated, Charles Pittman was working as a newspaper publisher at Lee Enterprise Inc. of Davenport, Iowa. For six years he
served as a senior vice president of the fourth largest newspaper chain in
America, publishing fifty-four newspapers in twenty-three states. In June
2002 he was told to find twenty jobs he could cut to reduce costs and improve the company's bottom line. He wanted to consider other cost-cutting
options that wouldn't leave loyal employees without jobs, but he was told
he needed to execute the order. Rather than do so, he quit as a matter of
principal.

"Now where do you think I learned those principles?" said Pittman,
currently a vice president of Schurz Communications, publishers of the
South Bend Tribune in Indiana. The answer is Penn State and Joe Paterno.
Pittman learned to get the best out of himself on the football field and
beyond. Paterno taught him that his word must be impeccable and that a
manager's most important task was to remove obstacles that stand in an
employee's way, not to boss him around or do his job for him. As one who
had been recruited in the original class of the Grand Experiment, Pittman learned the Paterno Way and took what he learned into the business
world: "I didn't understand all the things he was teaching us, but as you
grow older, I understood that he was preparing us for life beyond the football field." Joe Paterno considered himself to be a teacher first and a coach

second. He wanted everyone he had a chance to mentor to strive for personal excellence.

Jack Ham, a linebacker from Johnstown, Pennsylvania, was another early recruit for the Grand Experiment. Ham received a scholarship in 1967 after another recruit turned it down. He went on to become one of the greatest linebackers ever to perform for Penn State, earning All-American status while playing on teams that were a combined 29–3 in his three seasons as a starter.

"Joe's order of priorities was family, education, and football," Ham said in an interview. "He said the only time you get into trouble is when you get those things out of order. The thing I remember most is that he always told us not to think we were something special because we were football players. To him, football was an extracurricular activity, and we were all part of the university. Joe didn't believe in separate dorms for football players. We were mixed in with the student population."

By Ham's senior season, Jerry Sandusky had taken over as the defensive coach in charge of linebackers. But Paterno, the dominant voice on the team, told Sandusky not to overcoach the young player. The defense and offense conducted their practice drills on adjoining fields, with Paterno noticing every detail in both places and making adjustments in his high-pitched Brooklyn accent if things weren't to his liking.

"If you heard him scream, it would put the fear of God into you," Ham said. "Everybody on those practice fields knew where he was. You had to have your head on a swivel, like Linda Blair in *The Exorcist*. You didn't know who he was screaming at, but you hoped it wasn't you. He was a big believer in preparation. He was a tough disciplinarian because he really cared about us as people. He used to say that you either get better or you get worse every day. Fun time was Saturday, when we played the games."

Ham went on to have a stellar career with the Pittsburgh Steelers. He played on four Super Bowl championship teams, and in 1988 was elected to the Pro Football Hall of Fame. For his induction, Ham asked Paterno to be his presenter. "Joe did more for me than anybody in my career," he said. "I was just a kid looking for an opportunity, and he gave me that opportunity."

Matt Bahr was an atypical example of what it was like to play for Paterno. Bahr was an electrical engineering major and a soccer player when Paterno asked him to be his kicker. "The thing with Joe was that school came first," Bahr said in a recent interview. "You weren't going to be part of the team unless you had good grades. To him, football was part of the journey, not the destination. Education led to opportunities. He wasn't concerned about guys playing football. He was concerned about their ability to earn a living after graduation. I was like every kid up there. I enjoyed the college experience, got the most out of my education, and made friends for life."

But Bahr still remembers those practices and hearing that Brooklyn accent when things weren't up to Joe's standards. "I might miss a field goal from two hundred yards away," he said, exaggerating for emphasis, "and he would come running up and yell, 'Aw nuts! Bahr, you stink.' I still get goose bumps to this day thinking about that voice. He wasn't an easy coach to play for. He was very demanding. No matter what your best was, he expected you to get better. But we all appreciated what he did for us."

Bahr, now a design engineer in Pittsburgh, was an All-American at Penn State and played sixteen seasons in the National Football League, including stints with the Pittsburgh Steelers, San Francisco 49ers, and New York Giants. "I have fond memories of the football program at Penn State. Joe was one of the best coaches I ever knew."

Paterno's loyalty to Penn State was unwavering. In 1969, three years after he took over as head coach, he rejected an offer to coach the Pittsburgh Steelers. Four years later he verbally agreed to become head coach of the New England Patriots under a package that would pay him $1.4 million as coach, general manager, and part owner. It would be a huge jump in pay for a college coach raising a family of five on $35,000 a year. But on the day the deal was to become official, he called the Patriots' owner Billy Sullivan to say that he was staying put. In a story that he recounted a number of times over the years, Paterno said he told his wife, "You went to bed with a millionaire and you woke up with me. I'm not going."

Over the years Paterno was offered a number of coaching jobs, but he always turned them down. "I stayed because this is where I thought I would be happier, and where I could do more good."

Learning that Paterno had turned down the Patriots' offer, the Penn State student body elected him to give the school's commencement address that spring, 1973. Paterno told the graduates, "Money alone will not make you happy. Success without honor is an unseasoned dish. It will satisfy your hunger, but it won't taste good."

"Success with Honor" soon became the catchphrase of Penn State football. Paterno was a sympathetic figure in his early coaching days. He had unbeaten teams in 1968, 1969, and 1973, but he was never awarded a national title by the pollsters. The frustration of not being recognized boiled over after the 1973 season. Penn State, led by the Heisman Trophy winner John Cappelletti, was a perfect 12–0. They went on to beat Louisiana State in the Orange Bowl, but they still finished a disappointing fifth in the polls. A disgusted Paterno sought out the sports writers who covered his team and told them, "I had my own poll, the Paterno poll. And the vote was unanimous. Penn State is Number One. I took the vote a few minutes ago." He even had championship rings made for his players.

Then, in 1978, Penn State finally achieved the No. 1 ranking for the first time in its history. The only thing standing in the way of a national title was second-ranked Alabama, which was chosen as the Nittany Lions' opponent in the Sugar Bowl in New Orleans. Alabama won 14–7 as Penn State failed twice to score from the one-yard line in the closing minutes.

A breakthrough came during the 1982 season, when Paterno finally took Penn State to the top. Ranked second in the country, Penn State had a showdown with No. 1 Georgia in the Sugar Bowl. In the days leading up to the game, rival fans teased and taunted each other on Bourbon Street in the French Quarter. At a big New Year's Eve party at the media hotel, Paterno made a brief appearance as Pete Fountain's jazz band provided the background music.

During the festivities Paterno approached the media representatives to ask about the well-being of long-time Associated Press sports writer Ralph Bernstein, who was forced to make an emergency return to Philadelphia because his wife had been murdered. The day before the biggest game of his coaching career, he wanted to let the Bernstein family know his thoughts were with them. Penn State won the game 29–23. The defense, coached by Jerry Sandusky, largely shut down Georgia's running back Herschel Walker to preserve the win. Finally, after all those years, Penn State was No. 1. Players hoisted Paterno onto their shoulders and carried him off the field. The Grand Experiment had succeeded.

But as proud as Paterno was of the team's victory, he made sure to talk about classroom achievements as much as football achievements. Todd Blackledge, the winning quarterback, was a Phi Beta Kappa. Better known today as a football broadcaster than for his career in the National Football League, Blackledge had a 3.83 grade point average out of a possible 4.0. Also on that team were three Academic All-Americans. The graduation rate for players that year was 90 percent, higher than for the overall student population at Penn State. "These players aren't put in any easy classes," Paterno said. "They have to work at it because that is the only way to get anything out of a university. Most of the people we recruit will accept that challenge. There is no sense in being involved in something unless you want it to be the best. I really believe there is something more to a college football experience than winning or losing. If after four years a kid leaves and he hasn't learned anything from me, it's been a tragic waste, for both of us."

IN THE GLORY DAYS OF the Roman Empire, a conquering general would be paraded along the Via Sacra to the cheers of the adoring mob. A slave following the conqueror would repeat a warning: "You are mortal. You are mortal. You are mortal." After the Sugar Bowl victory, as the Penn State football team rode in coach buses from the Harrisburg airport back to State College, two hours away, the champions were saluted by people in every small town along U.S. Route 322. Occasionally the buses were escorted by local fire company trucks with lights flashing and sirens wailing. One church put a sign on its billboard with the message, "These Christians Root for the Lions."

The procession finally reached campus after midnight, greeted by a throng of celebratory students and townies. Trophy in hand, Paterno led them in a chant. "We are Penn State!" he crowed. At future home games, at the urging of cheerleaders, half the crowd at Beaver Stadium would yell "JOE-PA!" and the other half would respond "TERNO!" The nickname JoePa had been born.

Penn State lost a bid to win a second national championship following the 1985 season, when the Nittany Lions were beaten by Oklahoma in the Orange Bowl. But in 1986, the 100th season of football at Penn State, the Paterno legend reached new heights. Ranked second in the country, Penn State beat heavily favored No. 1 Miami in the Sunkist Fiesta Bowl. Bowl officials asked NBC-TV to move the game to Friday, January 2, 1987, to get better ratings; it was the first time a bowl game was played after New Year's Day. On Paterno's directive, Penn State players arrived for the game wearing coats and ties, while Miami players donned combat fatigues. Miami's coach Jimmy Johnson referred to Paterno at a news conference as "Saint Joe." Paterno had already been recognized as Sportsman of the Year by *Sports Illustrated,* which said his combination of high graduation rates and football success made him "stick out like a clean thumb."

Penn State won the game 14–10 in Jerry Sandusky's finest hour as defensive coordinator. The Lions recovered a pair of fumbles and had five interceptions, the last one a game-saving interception with eighteen seconds to play. Once again victorious players lifted JoePa onto their shoulders and carried him off the field in triumph. At the age of sixty, he was on top of the world, the new Lion King.

Penn State gave up its status as an independent football power and began competing in the Big Ten Conference in 1993. The switch coincided with a new endorsement deal from Nike, which provided Penn State with uniforms and shoes, and in 1995 the Nike swoosh appeared on the team's jerseys. The deal was worth more than $2 million to the university. But not everybody was pleased with the commercialism of the deal. When Keith Jackson, a Hall of Fame football announcer, saw the new look he said, "That's like the Mona Lisa having a mustache."

In its first thirty-four seasons under Paterno, Penn State had only one losing season. The winning ways changed in 2000, one year after Sandusky retired as defensive coordinator. In the next five years the Nittany Lions had four losing seasons. Whether it was coincidence or Sandusky meant that much to the program, Penn State football entered into what fans called the Dark Ages. Penn State's overall record during that time was 26–33.

In addition to problems on the playing field, there were off-field issues as well. In 2003 alone, eleven Penn State players were cited or arrested for violations ranging from alcohol abuse to sexual assault. Some alumni and media columnists called for Paterno to step down for the good of the program. For years Paterno had talked about not wanting to stay too long, but he always kept going. "What am I going to do? Cut the grass?" he said repeatedly.

At the end of the 2004 season Paterno, now seventy-eight, invited high-ranking administrators at Penn State to his house. He felt it was finally time to step down. The group included President Graham Spanier, Athletic Director Tim Curley, Senior Vice President of Finance Gary Schultz, and Steve Garban, chairman of the board of trustees. Garban had been a Nittany Lions captain when Engle was coach and Paterno was his assistant.

The meeting took place at Paterno's kitchen table, the same table where Mike McQueary sat in 2002 to tell the coach about Sandusky and the shower incident. Discussions were held on an orderly transition, as well as who Paterno's successor would be. The group reconvened several times in the next several days. Eventually Paterno told Spanier he wanted his successor to be Tom Bradley, the defensive coordinator who had taken over when Sandusky retired. The group authorized Spanier to sound out Bradley about the possibility. Before Bradley was contacted, however, Paterno changed his mind. He decided he was going to stay and turn the program around. Nobody in the inner circle challenged him. Was there any doubt who was the ultimate authority at Penn State?

Penn State's football fortunes did rebound. From 2005 to the start of the 2010 season the Nittany Lions had a 58–19 record, won two more Big Ten Conference championships, and appeared in five more bowl games, winning four of them.

In December 2007, at a black-tie dinner at the Waldorf-Astoria in New

York City, Paterno was inducted into the College Football Hall of Fame. He said at a news conference, "I appreciate the fact that people have said, 'Hey, you've been an asset to college football and we want to acknowledge that.' I've tried to be good for college football. I'm not saying I'm the best coach. But I've worked hard to be good, because I really love college football."

Paterno's love of the game was never in question. But the activities of his long-time assistant coach, long retired from his staff, would entangle the university and Paterno himself in the biggest sex scandal ever to hit college sports.

CHAPTER SEVEN

———

THE BEGINNING OF THE
END OF SANDUSKY

From the start of her eleven-year-old son's involvement in The Second Mile, a young single mother from Clinton County, Pennsylvania, thought the charity would provide a great opportunity for him; she hoped he would benefit from the self-image programs and positive direction it provided. The Second Mile's objective of elevating the attitudes and changing the outlooks of troubled kids could help a child like hers. When Jerry Sandusky took a special interest in her son, who had no male presence in his life, she was even more pleased. The man was a celebrity in central Pennsylvania, where Penn State football was like a religion. He was an icon, the mastermind of the defenses that translated into great victories. Young children proudly and dutifully wore the school's blue-and-white gear. The venerated founder of the charity was also bringing former Nittany Lions stars, elite pro football players, and other professional athletes to The Second Mile programs. All the athletes were eager to work with troubled children. The mother had no idea that Sandusky had been accused twice before of inappropriate sexual contact with young boys.

She was a single mother raising two children, a son and a daughter. A school counselor had referred her son to The Second Mile. The first three years of his involvement with the charity were all good, as far as she knew. He had become fond of Sandusky, and they developed a close relationship. The boy thoroughly enjoyed the gifts he received from his mentor. He also gained entry into the exclusive world of Penn State football because of his Sandusky connection. While some of the affectionate attention unnerved him, eventually he was able to accept words of love and devotion from Sandusky, even if at times they made him uncomfortable. There were times when his mother became somewhat concerned at Sandusky's behavior, thinking his attention was too friendly. She found it disconcerting that Sandusky would sometimes show up unannounced to pick up her child at his school bus stop, supposedly so they could chat. When the boy misbehaved, she noticed Sandusky trying to take over her role as a parent. She chose to let those issues go, however, because of the benefits her child was getting from his association with The Second Mile and Sandusky.

Eventually the relationship became too much for the child. The mother listened to vague complaints about how controlling Sandusky was, but figured they stemmed from the streak of independence most children experience as they enter their teenage years. Her concern grew when the child told her he wanted to pull back from the relationship with the man.

The comments from her son became more and more emphatic and alarming. Even when he had stopped attending Second Mile events, he told her Sandusky kept visiting him at school. Her concerns turned into action one evening when the child said he wanted to look up "sex weirdoes" on the Internet in almost the same breath that he mentioned Sandusky. She called officials at Central Mountain High to ask just how often Sandusky visited her child there. When she learned Sandusky spent an inordinate amount of time with him, often in private one-on-one situations during and after school without her permission, she asked them to discreetly question her son about the relationship.

On a Friday in the spring of 2008, the young mother was summoned to the principal's office at the rural high school. She found her son weeping and curled up in a fetal position in a chair. She was horrified to learn that he had broken down and admitted that the founder of The Second Mile charity had been sexually abusing him for years. The more she learned about her son's allegations, the worse she felt. When she pressed him about why he hadn't told her what was happening to him, he said he was afraid of Sandusky and also feared that no one would believe him. "Well, I didn't know what to do," he said. "You just can't tell Jerry no."

The distraught mother didn't know what to do either, but her first re-action was to demand that school officials call the police. At the time she didn't know they were obliged by state law to report allegations of child abuse within forty-eight hours. But instead of telling her they would report Sandusky, she said they asked her to go home and consider her options over the weekend before making a decision. She was outraged. Her child was having an emotional breakdown over having to admit being sexually abused by Sandusky, and school officials seemed more concerned about Sandusky's reputation than they were about him. Once home she angrily called a friend who worked in social services and quickly made a report of her own that ultimately landed on the desk of the Clinton County district attorney.

At the time no one at the school knew there were previous reports on Sandusky dating back almost a decade. In fact, Sandusky showed up to volunteer as a football coach at Central Mountain High just months after he had been barred from bringing The Second Mile kids around the Penn State football program. The Second Mile's chairman of the board, John Raykovitz, had been made aware of that probe, as well as the one from 1998.

Pennsylvania law dictates that anyone in contact with children in a school must undergo a detailed criminal background check. It is unclear if Sandusky provided one, but the former coach would have passed muster anyway because the earlier incidents were either unsubstantiated or never reported.

Central Mountain High officials were familiar with Sandusky long before he volunteered to coach football there. Several other children who used the services of The Second Mile went to school there. For years Sandusky made frequent trips to the school to counsel his charges, many of whom were in and out of trouble. School administrators and coaches alike considered him to be a nice guy with a heart of gold. They felt honored that a man with his coaching pedigree and concern for children would give so much of himself, especially since the kids he nurtured needed it the most.

By the time the mother brought to everyone's attention the alleged dark side of Sandusky, her son had enjoyed two years of his "kindness." The renowned coach would single him out and take him aside at The Second Mile camps on the Penn State campus to help him improve his running form and other athletic skills. At the time Sandusky wasn't even supposed to be on campus with young children. Also at Penn State, Sandusky would take the boy to preseason practices, allowing him to patrol the sidelines as if he belonged in the rarified football family. Sandusky took him to Philadelphia to see the Eagles play, and to college games. The child was invited to stay overnight in a basement bedroom at the Sandusky home.

Sandusky created an emotional bond with the child by lavishing him with gifts his single mother would never have been able to afford. There were golf clubs, a computer, gym and dress clothes, and cash. The boy ate with Sandusky at restaurants, went swimming with him at an area hotel. He even attended church with the Sandusky family. The mother meanwhile was becoming more certain that the founder of the charity was going far beyond the group's mission. She found out later that on nights her child stayed at the Sandusky home, the man would come into the darkened basement bedroom late at night offering to crack the boy's back. That story would prove to describe the same grooming process Sandusky allegedly used repeatedly against others. The child said Sandusky would enter his basement room, get into bed with him, and then roll around until he was face-to-face on top of him. Sandusky would run his arms along the child's back to "crack" it, something he did almost every time the child visited. As the child was preparing to enter the sixth or seventh grade, Sandusky started the practice of blowing on his stomach. Soon, the boy said, he began kissing him on the mouth, which caused the youngster to become so uncomfortable he would try to hide in the basement to avoid him. In 2007, the boy claimed, the oral sex began. The child said Sandusky performed oral sex on him about twenty times between 2007 and 2008, and forced him to do it in return once. He said that Sandusky also repeatedly touched him inappropriately.

Tormented by feelings of self-hatred and shame, the child decided he had to get away from him. In 2008, entering his freshman year at Central Mountain High, he stopped taking calls from his Sandusky and told his mother to tell the man he wasn't home when he stopped by. Unfortunately, by that time Sandusky had become firmly entrenched in his position as a volunteer assistant football coach at Central Mountain High, so it was impossible to avoid him entirely. He was always around, either coaching football during the fall season or overseeing conditioning programs during the rest of the year. He was also mentoring several kids in the school district school through The Second Mile, which gave him access to the school buildings. He was so trusted by administrators that they permitted him to pull kids out of class and take them away from the school for what he told administrators were counseling sessions.

There was a witness to Sandusky's inappropriate behavior, the boy said. About a year before he began trying to distance himself from Sandusky in earnest, the two had been alone in the school's weight room. The boy said he had been attempting to climb the school's rock wall, but kept falling. After one failed effort, when he was still sprawled on the safety mat, Sandusky lay down face-to-face on top of him, then began rolling around with him. When they stopped rolling, Sandusky embraced the child for a period of time with his eyes closed. Joseph Miller, the elementary school's wrestling coach, was retrieving something in the area when he noticed a light on in the weight room. He walked in and saw the two lying side-by-side in close contact. Sandusky immediately jumped up and said sheepishly, "Hey coach, we're just working on wrestling moves."

Miller found the situation puzzling. He knew Sandusky was not a wrestling coach, and he wondered why they would be alone in that secluded area when a much larger wrestling room was nearby. The child let Sandusky do the talking. The boy said he had repeatedly been threatened to keep the relationship quiet. He also said he had been warned that no one would believe him if he did tell the truth about what was going on.

Miller would not say anything about what he saw for almost two years. Like the rest of the Central Mountain High community, he knew Sandusky's reputation as a man who was firm but fair with troubled kids. Shouting matches between Sandusky and the most troubled angry children were not uncommon on school grounds, because, it was believed, he wanted more from the kids than they were willing to give. Sandusky was given the benefit of the doubt in his interactions with the young people, in no small part because he was so respected as an honorable, well-intentioned substitute father figure.

Steven Turchetta, the head football coach and assistant principal at Central Mountain High, and a passionate Penn State football fan, was elated when Sandusky came to coach for free. He had only admiration for Sandusky's work with kids, especially evident with the few of them who played on the football team. Like other administrators there, he was not alarmed by the fact that several students were allowed to be alone with Sandusky on school grounds and elsewhere. Yet despite his confidence in Sandusky, he would later characterize him as "very controlling within the mentoring relationships he established with The Second Mile students." Turchetta knew from his own experience that schisms between coaches and kids were not that extraordinary. Sometimes he'd act as a mediator in spats between recalcitrant Second Mile kids and the volunteer coach.

Something suspicious Turchetta noted in hindsight was Sandusky's behavior when a child from The Second Mile program seemed to be rejecting him. Turchetta described Sandusky's demeanor at those times as "clingy" and "needy."

For this boy, who was trying to escape Sandusky, having him cruising the halls of Central Mountain High was a nightmare. By this point his mother knew that he wanted nothing more to do with Sandusky, but she did not know why. She was concerned that he felt so repulsed by him, but kept her concerns to herself, still believing Sandusky had only good intentions. Her son had not yet told her that school officials liberally granted Sandusky permission to pull him from a late afternoon study hall for unmonitored meetings in a conference room, and occasionally even took him off school property. When the youngster finally told his mother about the abundant contacts with Sandusky at Central Mountain High, she called the school principal and the guidance counselor. "If nothing else, he's taking my son out of classes and leaving the school with him," she complained. According to what she told a reporter from the Harrisburg *Patriot-News,* she then asked the principal if he'd be willing to summon her son to his office in order to ask him how he felt about Sandusky. Shortly thereafter she herself was called to the office, where she found her son in tears.

The boy had already admitted that Sandusky had been molesting him for years. "I'm infuriated," his mother said in the newspaper interview. "Even if they had the slightest inclination that anything inappropriate was going on it should have been reported, or at least brought to my attention. I didn't even know he was leaving the school with my child, taking him out of classes. They never told me that." Both the mother and school officials reported Sandusky to the appropriate authorities, and Sandusky was immediately barred from the campus. Still, no one in the legal system seemed to know what to do with the complaint. While some of the abuse clearly occurred on high school property, the complaint was originally referred from Clinton County to nearby Centre County, where Sandusky lived and where the child said he was repeatedly assaulted.

In March 2009 Centre County District Attorney Michael Madeira passed the matter to the state attorney general. Madeira had very little information about the 1998 complaint against Sandusky, and knew nothing about the 2002 allegations. In passing the matter to the state attorney general's office, he cited a conflict of interest because one of Sandusky's adopted children was related to his wife. Pennsylvania Attorney General Tom Corbett sent the matter to the state police, where the case was assigned to an investigator, Corporal Joe Leiter, who was based in central Pennsylvania. This time officials at Penn State had no control over the investigation. Unlike in the past, this time investigators would seek out others with stories similar to this boy's, even if putting together the dark puzzle of the former coach's alleged secret life would be a monumental challenge.

CHAPTER EIGHT

THE INVESTIGATION WIDENS

Corporal Joe Leiter of the Pennsylvania State Police had a gut feeling that Jerry Sandusky might be a serial sexual predator. In the spring of 2008 he had just finished his first round of interviews with the fifteen-year-old boy from Central Mountain High who claimed that Sandusky had sexually abused him for almost four years. What struck Leiter about the child's story was the way he had been lured into trusting the former football coach. Sandusky showered him with attention, then gifts, then special trips; then the abuse began. The pattern was typical of pedophiles, right down to the part where the abuser kept the boy quiet by convincing him nobody would believe him if he told. The officer suspected that this boy was not Sandusky's only victim.

Leiter, a Centre County native, had been a state trooper for twenty-four years and was the supervisor of the crime unit in his jurisdiction. Normally his caseload did not include sex crimes, but ranged from aggravated assault to drug trafficking. Leiter was also a popular volunteer in youth programs in the Bellefonte area, although his work was not affiliated with The Second Mile.

The boy and his sister trusted Leiter, with his gentle and reassuring manner. The two gave the corporal the names of a few of their classmates and other youngsters they knew who participated in The Second Mile programs. Most of the kids in the charity program knew each other only by their first names, making it harder to identify potential witnesses. A lot of the last names Leiter was given turned out to be wrong.

Leiter learned that Sandusky had written an autobiography, *Touched: The Jerry Sandusky Story,* published in 2001 by Sports Publishing LLC, an Illinois-based vanity press that specialized in books about professional and college sports. Sandusky had written the book the year he retired from Penn State. The paperback was still available at the Penn State bookstore.

Leiter read Sandusky's own words about how his intense love for children had inspired him to start The Second Mile. He learned that the coach was proud of the way he reached out to help kids. One particular passage that jumped out at Leiter was Sandusky's admission that he relished engaging in risky behavior. "These were the perils I faced as a youngster," Sandusky wrote. "I did so because I thrived on testing the limits of others, and I enjoyed taking chances in danger." The book continued, "I had a personal law—Jer's law—that I stuck to when I was growing up and I still abide by that law today. I allowed myself to be mischievous, but I didn't let it get to the point that someone would be intentionally hurt . . . and I swore I would tell the truth if I was ever caught doing something wrong. That law has certainly been tested through the years, and just because it is a law doesn't mean it has kept me out of trouble."

Other chapters in the book listed the first names of about a dozen young participants in The Second Mile, and Sandusky had seen fit to publish photos of himself surrounded by some of the boys with whom he had forged close relationships. With this information Leiter had a place to start. He showed the names and photos to the boy from Central Mountain High to see if he recognized anyone or knew the last names of any of the kids. With one name provided by the boy, Leiter located a young man who had been a witness to inappropriate behavior. He said he had seen Sandusky rubbing a boy's leg while a few of the Second Mile boys were in his car driving to an Eagles game in Philadelphia. Leiter coaxed out a few more names of youngsters particularly close to Sandusky. Armed with names and addresses, he began knocking on their doors to ask if they knew anything about questionable conduct on Sandusky's part, and whether they had experienced something personally.

Finally, a young man who answered the door had critical information to share. "How did you find me?" he asked.

Leiter explained the process of picking up clues in Sandusky's autobiography. The young man had never told anyone about his physical relationship with Sandusky, and he had hoped to keep the shameful episode buried forever. Even recalling the abuse to the detective meant reliving all the pain. Still, he opened up about trusting Sandusky as a loving and caring father figure before he was betrayed. At first his experience in The Second Mile had been positive. He felt that Sandusky genuinely cared about him because of the attention, gifts, and access to the Penn State football games that he provided. All the while Sandusky pushed the boundaries of hugging and touching and wrestling up to the time the young man felt overpowered by him and succumbed to his advances. The young man told Leiter that once the sexual abuse started, he felt trapped. He loved the affection and the gifts, but he was shamed by the price he had to pay, again and again, during the course of several years. Then Sandusky suddenly stopped coming around.

Leiter now had a corroborating story to support the accusations of the boy from Central Mountain High. In essence, Jerry Sandusky's own book had provided the investigator with a road map back to himself.

From this young man Leiter learned the identities of more potential victims. One by one, reluctant young men described to Leiter a side of Sandusky the public never saw. The stories were remarkably similar. It became clear to Leiter that Sandusky had formulated a consistent game plan, just as he had done as the coach for thirty-two years on the Penn State football staff. Leiter kept private the stories from others involved in The Second Mile when he conducted his interviews, making sure not to taint the case by tipping anyone off. He was the first investigator to lead a probe of San-

dusky's behavior who was not affiliated with Penn State. He had no alle-
giance to the university or the former defensive mastermind.

By late 2010 Leiter had gathered a remarkable number of accounts with
similar modus operandi from young men who claimed Sandusky had forced
himself on them sexually. According to these accounts, Sandusky, while
projecting a saintly image to the public, was preying on the vulnerabilities
of those assigned to his care. Few of them had male role models in their
lives, so all of them had been elated when a man of Sandusky's stature had
shown interest in them. He was a famous football coach and humanitarian
who invited them into a world they had no access to before. They had the
chance to meet real football players, associate with legends like Joe Paterno, and be in the mix of big-time college football. The family members
of the accusers had been fooled as well. Many were single parents grateful
that a man like Jerry Sandusky was helping their child, making them less
likely to see the affectionate attention negatively.

Leiter's investigation revealed that Sandusky had carefully observed
the young men for as long as two years before he made his move. According
to Leiter, he would seek targets with no adult male figures in their lives. He
would lavish them with gifts and words of love and affection like they had
never experienced before. He had them believing he genuinely cared for
them, and that they were special. Eventually he would encourage them to
join him in one-on-one workouts and other activities where they could be
alone. In almost every instance, Leiter's investigation indicated, Sandusky
would test them to gauge a response. If he could get away with rubbing
their leg in his car on the way to an event, he would push the boundaries
further. If the young men objected to the touching, Leiter reasoned, they
would not get any personal attention from him again, sexual or otherwise.
Those who didn't protest against the advances would remain in his good
graces, some for as long as four years. And they were all afraid to tell anyone
about what was going on, even their closest friends.

As the number of accusers grew, Leiter told his bosses he needed help.
By early 2011 seven investigators had been added to the team, coming from
both the attorney general's office and the state police department. It didn't
take long before everybody realized that officials from both Penn State and

The Second Mile had known about Sandusky's activities for years but had not stopped him. Sandusky had been caught twice showering with minors in the Penn State football locker room, and yet no substantive action had ever been taken.

The investigation by Penn State police into the 1998 incident came to light when the independent investigators learned that Sandusky had admitted to bear-hugging a young boy in the Penn State locker room showers. Searching the Internet for information about Sandusky, investigators found a short reference in a blog suggesting a graduate assistant in the football program had actually witnessed Sandusky molesting a child in a locker room shower in 2002. The blog led them to Mike McQueary, who reluctantly agreed to lend his voice to the investigation.

Eventually ten young men agreed to come forward and tell their stories under oath. Each young man had a horrendous account to share. There was a young man known as Sandusky's "favorite" at The Second Mile, who claimed the coach had assaulted him numerous times at Penn State's Holuba Hall football facility, at Sandusky's home, and at two different bowl games he attended with the coach and his family.

Detectives also tracked down the earliest case of abuse they could identify, one that dated back to 1994 and involved a ten-year-old boy sent to The Second Mile by a school counselor. As in the other cases, Sandusky had invested years in building a relationship with the boy and his family. Sandusky got the mother's permission to take her son to a State College High School football game that his son was going to play in. The child stayed the night at the Sandusky house, again with his mother's permission, and the next day his entire family joined the Sanduskys for a Penn State tailgate party and football game. The child enjoyed everything about the activities, especially the Penn State games. He was allowed to walk on the field during the contests, a coveted privilege reserved only for high-ranking insiders in Happy Valley. Sometimes he'd have breakfast with the coach. On occasion he even got to sit in on the coach's pregame meetings. Eventually boundaries were blurred. Sandusky started putting his hand on the boy's thigh as they were driving in his Cadillac, the boy said. The touching continued even after they pulled into the coach's two-car garage. Feeling uncomfortable, the boy tried to stop the advances by sitting as far away from Sandusky as possible when he was in the car. On more than one occasion, the boy claimed that Sandusky put his hands down the boy's pants, but the boy pulled away every time.

Another Second Miler told the detective he had also experienced improper touching in the car. That child initially didn't allow Sandusky's advances, but things changed when he stayed in the coach's basement bedroom. Sandusky would show up in the dead of night and cuddle him. He claimed the coach repeatedly bear-hugged him, ostensibly to crack his back. He told the investigators he had a "blurry memory" of other physical contact with Sandusky, and that he stopped seeing the man to avoid the sexual advances. He had kept the secret for almost fifteen years, letting it out only when the investigator knocked on his door. The young man had had no contact with Sandusky for many years, but in the weeks before he was scheduled to tell his story to a grand jury in 2011, he was contacted by Sandusky, his wife, and a friend of their family. All three left messages on his answering machine saying they wanted to talk with him about an important matter. He did not return those phone calls.

Another young man, now twenty-two years old, told Leiter and other investigators that he met Sandusky through The Second Mile in 1995 or 1996, when he was just eight. He was invited to attend Penn State football games and enjoy all the amenities that came with seeing a game for free. He said he attended as many as fifteen such events as Sandusky's guest. Traveling with the coach to attend professional football games, he had to endure the coach's hand on his leg any time he was in the front seat of the Cadillac. He said Sandusky also took him to the East Area locker rooms of Holuba Hall, brought him into a sauna, and jostled him around. He said Sandusky "would press his chest and body up against his back and then push him away." After the sauna Sandusky would tell him they needed to shower. He said he went to a distant shower and turned his back on Sandusky before he "looked over his shoulder and saw that Sandusky was looking at him with an erection," which the child did not understand at the time. He tried to ignore the coach. The next thing he knew, Sandusky's body touched him from behind and the man began rubbing the child's arms and shoulders. The child tried to slip away before Sandusky pinned him against a corner wall, took the child's hand, and placed it on his erect penis. Extremely uncomfortable, the child pulled Sandusky's hand away, left the shower, toweled himself off, got dressed, and asked the coach to take him home. He never let Sandusky touch him again, and he was never invited to another football game or special event. He never told anyone about Sandusky's behavior. He didn't learn until much later that just months before he had been accosted, Sandusky had promised police and a welfare department investigator that he would never shower with a child again.

Another young man the police located had been between seventh and eighth grade in 2000 when he met Sandusky. He had been involved with The Second Mile for two years when the coach began inviting him to football games, to his home, and to private workouts at Penn State facilities. They would exercise, and like the others, the child sought to stay far away from Sandusky in the shower. When the coach made him feel bad about distancing himself, he moved closer, and the coach patted him down, rubbed his shoulders with soap, washed his hair, and held him close with bear hugs. The boy said Sandusky was sexually aroused during one of the hugs from behind. He also slept in Sandusky's basement bedroom, where the coach would give him shoulder rubs, blow on his stomach, and tickle him on the inside of his thigh. He claimed Sandusky touched his genitals twice through his shorts, but he turned over on his stomach to stop him.

Despite Sandusky's promises two years earlier to never shower with children again, detectives would learn of another unreported allegation against Sandusky in the Lasch Building shower. Penn State janitorial staff who worked there told them they witnessed what appeared to be the assault of a young child by Sandusky in a shower. It was on a Friday night after Penn State's football team had gone on the road for an away game. Sandusky may have believed the facility would be empty because virtually everyone associated with Penn State football traveled with the team; he apparently didn't realize janitors were still on duty. Shortly after Sandusky got there, a janitor named Jim Calhoun heard a noise in the showers of the Lasch Building. He found a naked Sandusky with a boy who appeared to be no more than thirteen years old pinned against the wall. Shocked, Calhoun immediately went to look for his coworker, Ronald Petrosky. Before he could find him, Petrosky arrived; under the partition he could see two sets of feet, one of an adult, another of a child. He waited for a few minutes for them to finish showering. Then Sandusky, a man he recognized, walked out hand-in-hand with a young child. Both were carrying gym bags and had wet hair. He said Sandusky acknowledged him with a "Good evening." A few minutes later Calhoun finally found Petrosky and told him he had seen Sandusky naked in the shower, "holding the boy up against the wall and licking him." Calhoun had fought in the Korean War and had "seen people with their guts blown out, arms dismembered." Now he told Petrosky, "I just witnessed something in there I'll never forget." He also said he watched Sandusky perform oral sex on the child. Petrosky later told Leiter and others that Calhoun was so upset and agitated he feared the elderly janitor might have a heart attack. Calhoun had worked for Penn State for only eight months as an hourly day laborer. The two men were worried that if they reported what they had seen, they might be fired. Eventually Calhoun was persuaded to report the event to his supervisor, Jim Witherite. Witherite tried to calm Calhoun and told him how to properly report the incident, if he so chose. Calhoun valued his job over the possible consequences from telling on Sandusky, so he did nothing more at the time. Later that same evening Petrosky saw Sandusky sitting in a car in the parking lot outside the Lasch Building. At 10 P.M., Witherite confirmed it was Sandusky. Later, at almost midnight and again at around two o'clock, Petrosky saw Sandusky driving very slowly around and around the parking lot. Calhoun now suffers from dementia, lives in a nursing home, and is incompetent. Neither Witherite nor Petrosky nor Calhoun ever reported the incident to police or even to Penn State officials. While Witherite had asked the two men that night if they wanted to file an official report, Petrosky and Calhoun decided not to out of fear of losing their jobs. That child has never been identified.

Late in the investigation the detective found two more boys who said they were assaulted by Sandusky from 2004 to 2008 during a Second Mile swimming program. The first was eleven or twelve when Sandusky expressed an interest in spending time with him. As he had done with the others, Sandusky took him to Penn State games, lavished him with gifts, and gave him money. As the relationship developed, Sandusky would pick the child up from school on Friday afternoons so he could spend the night at Sandusky's home. That young man, who had little love in his life, called Sandusky a "very affectionate person." He thought of Sandusky as a nice guy. He even went to church with him. Then the touching began, which led to hugging and cuddling and tickling that before long degenerated into sexual assaults. The boy told investigators he also stayed in the basement bedroom of the Sandusky home, even though there were at least two empty upstairs bedrooms. Unlike the others, he said he even took his meals in the basement, brought to him by the former coach. He said he had stayed overnight many times at the Sandusky home over a three-year period, but had almost no contact with Sandusky's wife. She never came into the basement while he was there. The young man told investigators he had been forced to perform oral sex on Sandusky, and that Sandusky attempted anal rape against him at least sixteen times. There were times, he said, when Sandusky penetrated him. He had once screamed for help, knowing Sandusky's wife was upstairs, but no one had come to his aid. Sandusky also repeatedly took him to a State College-area hotel, where they would swim, sit in the Jacuzzi, and work out on exercise machines. During a few of the hotel visits, when there was no one else in the pool, he said Sandusky would expose his erect penis to him. On other occasions Sandusky had him perform oral sex on him at the hotel. Like most of the other accusers, this young man said Sandusky frequently told him that he loved and cared for him. Sandusky also told him to keep their encounters secret.

On March 31, 2011, another young man came forward after reading a story about the Sandusky investigation in the Patriot-News of Harrisburg. He called the Child Exploitation Tip Line, established by the state attorney general's office, to relay his story, and investigators were notified. The young man acknowledged that he had been a troubled child with a difficult home life when he started attending Second Mile functions at the age of ten. He met Sandusky in 1997 at a Second Mile camp, and the coach invited him to a Penn State football game. Sandusky picked him up at his house, took him to his own home for meals, and frequently lavished gifts on him. He told investigators Sandusky eventually created situations where they were alone so the coach could wrestle and cuddle with him in private. During one of those events, the coach pulled down his shorts and performed oral sex on him. The young man said the coach's act had startled him. But Sandusky repeated the abuse and eventually cajoled him into performing oral sex on him. He accused Sandusky of touching him indecently in the Penn State outdoor swimming pool, and said the coach would touch his genitals while he was tossing him around in the water. When Sandusky exposed himself and asked the child to perform oral sex on him as he was driving his car, he refused, and the friendship was over. The young man said he eventually told his stepmother that he no longer wanted anything to do with Sandusky, but did not tell her why.

The evidence the investigators gathered was as consistent as it was disturbing. As the time neared for all of the Second Mile participants to repeat their statements under oath before a grand jury, each young man thought he was the only one. It would not be until months after all of them told their stories that they would learn the magnitude of the allegations of Sandusky's serial sexual abuse of children.

CHAPTER NINE

COVER-UP

S ecrecy was the order of the day in late 2010, when the Thirty-third Statewide Investigating Grand Jury convened in the Harrisburg offices of Pennsylvania Attorney General Tom Corbett. In order to protect the integrity of the Sandusky investigation and the privacy of people called to testify, no public announcement was made about the meeting to be held in a room in the Strawberry Square offices of the attorney general. The twenty-three grand jurors and seven alternates who would weigh the case took an oath not to disclose matters occurring before them. The names of persons subpoenaed were not divulged to anyone beforehand, although after their testimony they had the right to speak to anyone of their choosing.

The grand jury system was perfectly suited for the Sandusky case. Investigators had collected a substantial list of young men who said they had been sexually assaulted by the coach. Other people who were going to testify had eyewitness accounts of Sandusky's activities. Prosecutors also wanted the panel to deliberate subtler issues, such as why Penn State of-

ficials didn't do more to stop Sandusky for almost a decade. Was it because they didn't want to tarnish the university's pristine image? Was it
a concerted cover-up? Were officials at Penn State telling the truth about
their actions? The prosecutors wanted grand jurors to hear answers to those
questions from as many witnesses as possible.

The prosecutors knew some of the accusers had emotional problems
or troubled pasts. Some of their stories were problematic too because they
were vague. The times and dates when abuse had occurred could not be
pinpointed. But when the ten young men delivered their first-person accounts, they impressed the grand jury with the similarities in their stories.

Assistant Coach Mike McQueary was the first independent witness to
say he personally saw Sandusky abusing a child in a football locker room
shower in 2002. He also provided a firsthand account of how university
officials failed to pursue legal action against the coach. When McQueary
testified, he did not know about the 1998 incident, in which Sandusky admitted showering with an eleven-year-old boy. Although Penn State police
and the Pennsylvania Department of Public Welfare had investigated the
claim in 1998, as in 2002 nothing of consequence was done about it.

During his testimony McQueary first explained the details of his view
of Sandusky's sexual assault. He believed the boy was a ten-year-old child.
He believed Sandusky was anally raping the boy, or at the very least was
sexually assaulting him. After he testified about the shower incident, Mc-
Queary told the grand jury he reported what he had seen to Joe Paterno.
He explained that Paterno told him he would send it up the chain of command, to Athletic Director Tim Curley and Vice President Gary Schultz,
the liaison with the school's police department. McQueary testified that
Curley told him that Sandusky would be barred from bringing children to
the football facilities and that the incident would be reported to officials of
The Second Mile charity.

THE GRAND JURY WAS STILL convened in early 2011 and hearing testimony when Penn State officials became aware that they might also be the
focus of the probe. They also knew as many as twenty Penn State employ-

ees had been interviewed by investigators. The officials had been told to expect grand jury subpoenas. Still, most believed that the Sandusky investigation had little to do with them. They thought that if they were called before the grand jury, they would be there as friendly witnesses, used to fill in the procedural blanks needed to paint a picture of how Sandusky could have used university facilities as a playground for sexual abuse.

Almost all of the Penn State witnesses were represented by a former Pennsylvania Supreme Court justice, Cynthia Baldwin, a Penn State graduate. Baldwin had served two years on the state's highest court to fill the term of a justice who had died, then had not sought retention. Prior to that, she had served as an Allegheny County common pleas judge in Pittsburgh. After her departure from the supreme court, she became chief legal counsel for Penn State.

On January 12, 2011, Baldwin and her clients, Joe Paterno, Tim Curley, and Gary Schultz, arrived at the courthouse in Harrisburg. Baldwin was present when prosecutors conducted pre-interviews with all of them. Normally this is the time when defense lawyers get an idea of the nature of what prosecutors are trying to determine. If lawyers believe their clients could incriminate themselves when they go in front of the grand jury, they will demand immunity for them. If immunity is not granted, lawyers can instruct their clients to refuse to testify under the U.S. Constitution's Fifth Amendment protections from self-incrimination. That day, however, neither Baldwin nor the three men thought there was a need for immunity.

Paterno was treated gingerly in his pre-interview. He did not want to be involved in explaining what he knew about Sandusky's actions in the football showers, especially because it could impact both Curley and Schultz, individuals he held in high regard. Despite his reticence, Paterno learned he would be asked only a limited number of questions about what McQueary had told him about the 2002 incident. Prosecutors also wanted to know what he had reported to others, and if he had any knowledge of the 1998 report by campus police. As long as he told the truth, they informed him, his appearance in the grand jury room would be very short. He then faced the panel by himself and was done in fourteen minutes.

During those fourteen minutes Paterno testified about what McQueary had told him at his kitchen table. He said the former quarterback did not describe lurid details, but he made it clear that Sandusky was seen "fondling, whatever you might call it, I'm not sure what the term would be . . . a young boy." He said it was of "a sexual nature." Paterno said he knew nothing about the 1998 shower incident. He also testified that he had never discussed anything about sexual misconduct with his former assistant coach, who retired in 1999. While Paterno and Sandusky had known each other for almost forty years, the coach said they were not close friends and rarely socialized together.

Before Curley's and Schultz's pre-interviews with prosecutors, they were unaware that they themselves had become a focus of the grand jury investigation. From the tone of the questions, however, they quickly realized the prosecutors were challenging their accounts of what actions they had taken with regard to the 2002 shower incident. Prosecutors believed the men had failed to report an incident of sexual abuse to proper authorities, a crime in Pennsylvania. Curley and Schultz both admitted they hadn't reported the matter to police and social service agencies, as required by Pennsylvania law, but contrary to what McQueary and Paterno had said, they had not been aware that sexual abuse had allegedly taken place. Despite the tone of the interviews, Baldwin did not request immunity for either of them.

Although Paterno's brief appearance had been relatively benign, first Curley and then Schultz were subjected to harsh questioning when they took the witness chair in the secret proceedings. Frank Fina, head of the attorney general's investigations branch, led the questioning. Fina walked both of them through the events of 2002, pointedly using the McQueary transcript. Fina was alleging the men had sanitized McQueary's report in their efforts to perpetrate a cover-up.

Curley was steadfast in his insistence that McQueary did not tell him there were sexual elements to the incident. As Fina vehemently pushed back with specific references to McQueary's testimony about what he called "the rape of a child" in the shower, the athletic director did not budge. "Absolutely not, he did not tell me that," Curley insisted.

"How would you characterize what McQueary told you?" Fina asked.

"I can't remember specifically, but my recollection is they were kind of wrestling, and were horsing around," Curley answered.

"Were they naked?" Fina asked.

"No," responded Curley.

"Was there sexual conduct?"

"No."

"At any time?"

"No."

For about forty minutes Curley repeatedly insisted that McQueary had not reported a case of sexual misconduct against Sandusky. He also denied knowing anything about the 1998 incident investigated by campus police. Fina was trying to get Curley to confirm his theory that inaction by top Penn State officials allowed Sandusky to abuse more children for almost a decade. Curley still didn't budge, and his lawyers would later say that he was telling the truth.

Schultz repeated much of the same when he followed Curley into the grand jury room. Unlike Curley, Schultz knew about the 1998 incident because his job responsibilities included oversight of the university police department. He said he told very few officials at Penn State about that incident because the Centre County district attorney declined to file charges and a state welfare official considered the allegation of abuse unfounded. He insisted that although the two reports four years apart had similar markings, the 1998 incident did not affect his decision-making process in 2002. He testified that since there were no overt allegations about a specific sexual assault in McQueary's report, he didn't report it to the Penn State police and never made an attempt to identify or question the child. When Fina confronted him with the details of McQueary's testimony, Schultz too insisted that McQueary never mentioned anything regarding a sexual assault. He said after he and Curley made a brief report to President Spanier, all of them agreed the proper solution was to order Sandusky not to bring young children into football facilities again and to report the incident to officials at The Second Mile charity. By the tone of the questioning it was clear to Schultz that Fina thought he was lying.

By the time they left the grand jury, Schultz and Curley realized they were the focus of an investigation for failing to properly report the 2002 incident. It also seemed that prosecutors thought they had lied before the grand jury about what McQueary had told them. Although in some instances witnesses are permitted to return to the grand jury to modify their statements, Baldwin did not ask for that opportunity for her clients. They left Harrisburg wondering whether their own words would be used against them. They would learn the answer to that about ten months later.

AS THE GRAND JURY INVESTIGATION progressed and more alleged accusers brought their stories before the panel, prosecutors continued to focus on a cover-up. The second case they pursued in that regard was the 1998 investigation against Sandusky. On March 10, 2011, every official related to that incident was brought before the grand jury. Among them was Detective Ronald Schreffler of the Penn State Police Department, who had led the month-long investigation into the accusations. Also testifying were Jerry Lauro of the Pennsylvania Department of Public Welfare, who worked with Schreffler on the probe, and Karen Arnold, a former assistant district attorney in Centre County, who handled child abuse cases for the office for many years. Before her testimony Arnold was specifically told that prosecutors were seeking evidence of a cover-up by Penn State officials, but she repeatedly told them she had no information of a cover-up. Her own boss, Ray Gricar, who had decided not to prosecute at the time of the 1998 investigation, had disappeared in 2005. Arnold told prosecutors she had little information about why Gricar had decided not to press charges.

When Detective Schreffler entered the grand jury room, he had in his possession the ninety-five-page report he had compiled. He testified that Ray Gricar had discounted the investigation in one conversation with him, insisting there was no evidence of sexual misconduct on the part of Sandusky.

Jerry Lauro, the welfare investigator, testified as to his role in the probe. He said Sandusky claimed the boy's mother misconstrued what was going on, and that the incident had not been sexual. In addition, back then a

mental health professional had reviewed the evidence provided by Schreffler and had determined that Sandusky did not match the profile of a sexual
predator.

Neither Arnold, Schreffler, nor Lauro provided the smoking gun that a
deliberate cover-up had taken place.

By the time Graham Spanier, the president of the university, was called
to testify, he was aware the *Patriot-News* of Harrisburg was preparing a
story saying Jerry Sandusky was the target of a grand jury investigation.
Spanier was also being represented by Cynthia Baldwin. He was one of
the few officials who agreed to appear before the grand jury without being
subpoenaed. Baldwin did not request immunity for him either.

Although Spanier was well aware of the extent of the grand jury probe
by the time he did his pre-interview with Deputy Attorney General Jonelle
Eshbach on March 22, he wasn't overly concerned. At that point it was
clear that the outcome of the investigation was not going to cast the university in a positive light, but he intended to be as helpful as possible. Spanier
considered himself to be a lifelong proponent of law enforcement; he saw
no reason to change that philosophy before the grand jury. For years he
had enjoyed top government security clearance through working with the
FBI as chair of the National Security Higher Education Advisory Board.
He had also worked with the National Counterintelligence Group in
Washington, D.C.

To Spanier, the pre-interview was relatively uneventful, filled with
questions about the operations of the university. As for Sandusky, Eshbach wanted to know what Spanier knew about the 2002 report by Mc-
Queary, when he knew it, and what he did about it. Spanier told Eshbach
essentially the same things Curley and Schultz had said. He had received
a nonspecific report from his underlings in 2002 about a staff member
who said Sandusky and a young child were "horsing around" or engaged
in "horseplay" in a football locker room shower. He said the senior officials
did not tell him the event involved sexual abuse, did not identify the staff
member, and did not tell him anything about the identity of the child. He
said he did not even know Sandusky and the child were naked. He told the
prosecutor Curley and Schultz told him about the incident in a short, un-

scheduled meeting at his Old Main office. Since the report did not appear to include criminality, Spanier said he quickly approved of their decision to ban Sandusky from bringing children to Penn State facilities and to report the inappropriate activity to The Second Mile's administrators. It was not referred to law enforcement because neither of his close associates believed criminality was involved.

When he made his appearance before the panel on April 13, Spanier expected his testimony would be about the workings of the university and the vague 2002 report Curley and Schultz had made to him. He did not know his underlings had become prime targets of the probe.

Eshbach casually asked him questions about rules concerning children on campus, the hours of access to Penn State's 1,700 buildings, and specifics about the Lasch Building, where many of the alleged assaults had occurred. Deputy Attorney General Frank Fina took over the questioning with a sterner tone. For the first time Spanier realized he was being asked questions that could implicate his aides in criminal activities, which he found abhorrent because he did not believe they had done anything wrong. He was aghast when Fina asked him angrily if he thought sodomy between a grown man and a boy in a Penn State football locker room shower was appropriate. Would he, the prosecutor wanted to know, insist on a full-scale investigation if he received a report about man-boy sodomy in a university shower? Spanier said that was the first time he'd heard of such a thing, but he most assuredly would sanction a probe under such circumstances. Not only had he himself been physically abused as a child, but he was trained as a family therapist, he said. He would never turn away from such information.

Fina walked him through the inconsistencies between what McQueary said under oath and the testimony from Curley and Schultz. Spanier reiterated what he had told Eshbach in the pre-interview: his underlings had told him the incident involved "horseplay" or "horsing around." He had not heard anything related to anal rape or sexual abuse. He didn't even know McQueary was the staff member who had made the report until the prosecutor divulged that information to him.

Spanier insisted that Schultz had never told him about the 1998 locker

COVER-UP   89

room shower incident involving Sandusky. He admitted that if he had
known about the earlier incident his reaction may have been different in
2002. When Fina questioned him about Sandusky's retirement shortly after
the 1998 incident, Spanier said he believed the former coach left the em-
ployment of the university because Paterno thought he was spending too
much time with the charity to do his job properly. He also said that Paterno had told Sandusky that he was not going to be his successor as head
coach. Specifically Spanier testified that he thought Sandusky left Penn
State because the State Employee Retirement System offered such a substantial early retirement incentive that the coach wanted to take advantage
of it. After Paterno gave him the bad news about his head coach prospects,
he saw no reason to stick around. Since Spanier claimed to know nothing
about the 1998 investigation into Sandusky, he could only deny any cause-
effect relationship between Sandusky's quiet exit and the 1998 report.

Spanier said he had not spoken to Curley or Schultz about their testimony, although he knew they had testified. In fact, he did not even tell
them he too was appearing before the secret panel.

When he left the grand jury that day, Spanier told his lawyer he felt he
had been sandbagged. Now he realized that the scope of the investigation
had been broadened to include questions about what Penn State officials
knew about Sandusky's conduct and what they had done about it. From the
tone of the questioning, it was clear prosecutors were pursuing evidence
of an illegal cover-up that had criminal implications for his trusted aides.
That, he told almost anyone who would listen, was not true. He feared the
prosecutors had not believed him.

As time passed with no action from the grand jury, Baldwin told
Spanier that they were nearing the eighteen-month point, when sessions
expire. If that happened without charges being announced, the case would
go away; prosecutors rarely presented evidence again to new grand juries.
On the first Saturday of November Spanier would learn that Baldwin was
patently wrong.

CHAPTER TEN
——

THE ARREST

Jerry Sandusky emerged into familiar surroundings when he stepped out of the backseat of a police car in handcuffs on November 5, 2011. The car was in a courthouse parking lot off West College Avenue, one of the main routes to Penn State University. Just across the street was the university's eighteen-hole Blue Course, one of two golf courses on the 17,000-acre campus. For three decades Sandusky had used the Penn State courses for his charity golf tournaments, which attracted big-name athletes and celebrities who participated in order to raise money for The Second Mile. During those tournaments Sandusky had ridden the fairways in a golf cart and always had a boy or two from The Second Mile with him. But golf and good times were the farthest things from his mind that Saturday morning. Escorted by two troopers and filmed by TV cameras, Sandusky was led into the courthouse to a district judge's office to be booked on criminal charges of sexually assaulting eight boys from The Second Mile over a thirteen-year period. Charges from two more accusers would be added

later. Once the charges were officially filed, Happy Valley would never be
the same.

Sandusky was brought before Magisterial Judge Leslie Dutchcot, a
contributor to and a volunteer at The Second Mile, whom he knew well.
The night before, he had been with family in Ohio. His son Jon was the
director of player personnel for the Cleveland Browns, and he had gone for
a visit. Now the heart and soul of the charity was standing in front of Judge
Dutchcot, charged with forty criminal counts ranging from involuntary de-
viate sexual intercourse to unlawful contact with a minor, endangering the
welfare of a child, corruption of minors, and indecent assault. The weighty
charges carried a maximum sentence of 565 years in prison and $600,000
in fines. Sandusky stood glum and silent during the ten o'clock proceedings.
He entered a plea of "not guilty" through his attorney, Joseph Amendola of
State College. Prosecutors had sought bail of $500,000. They assumed if
he made bail, he would be given an electronic ankle bracelet that would
alert authorities if he left his house. To their dismay, Sandusky was released
on $100,000 unsecured bond, which essentially meant he had to sign a
piece of paper to say that he would not flee and would show up for future
proceedings. No electronic monitoring device was ordered.

The reaction generated by Sandusky's arrest exploded beyond the sen-
sational. The biggest scandal in the history of college sports had cracked
open.

At the time of Sandusky's arraignment, the Pennsylvania attorney general's office in Harrisburg issued charges against two high-ranking Penn
State officials, Athletic Director Tim Curley and Senior Vice President for
Finance Gary Schultz. They each faced one count of perjury for making
false statements to a grand jury and for failing to abide by the Child Protec-
tive Services Law, which compels school officials to report suspected abuse
of children within forty-eight hours. They were to surrender in two days for
booking. If convicted, Curley and Schultz faced a maximum punishment of
seven years in prison and a $15,000 fine. Through their attorneys, both men
maintained their innocence.

A statement by Pennsylvania Attorney General Linda Kelly was posted
on the office's official website. The arrest confirmed the small-town rumors

that had been circulating for years and tore away the veil of secrecy that had concealed Sandusky's alleged dark side. Not only did Kelly lay out the criminal case for newspaper and media outlets; she alluded to a culture of silence that had covered it up: "This is a case about a sexual predator who used his position within the university and community to prey on young boys. It is also about high ranking university officials who allegedly failed to report the sexual assault of a young boy after it was brought to their attention, and later made false statements to a grand jury that was investigating a series of assaults on young boys."

Prosecutors emphasized the two incidents that had occurred on campus: the inappropriate behavior involving Sandusky and the eleven-year-old boy in the locker room shower in 1998, and the sexual assault of a ten-year-old boy in the locker room shower witnessed by Mike McQueary in 2002. The first investigation had been dropped without prosecution. In the 2002 incident, McQueary hadn't gone to police with his account, but he had contacted Coach Joe Paterno, who in turn had alerted the university officials Curley and Schultz. Prosecutors said there was no indication that anyone from the university had ever attempted to learn the identity of the ten-year-old boy in the 2002 case, or get his version of what had happened. But John Raykovitz, The Second Mile's CEO, had been notified of the 2002 incident. "The failure of top university officials to act on reports of Sandusky's alleged sexual misconduct, even after it was reported to them in graphic detail by an eyewitness, allowed a predator to walk free for years, continuing to target new victims," the attorney general added in her statement. "Equally disturbing is the lack of action and apparent lack of concern among those same officials, and others who received information about this case, who either avoided asking difficult questions or chose to look the other way."

Featured on the attorney general's website was the case of the Central Mountain High School student, whose allegations against Sandusky had sparked the in-depth investigation of the former coach by state police three years earlier. Even though the mother had complained that school officials were slow to act, the attorney general said they had immediately barred Sandusky from the school and reported the matter to authorities as required by state law: "The quick action by high school staff members in Clinton County in response to reports of a possible sexual assault by Sandusky is in marked contrast to the reaction of top officials at Penn State University, who had actually received a first-hand report of a sexual attack by Sandusky seven years earlier."

Although a news conference was scheduled for the Monday following the arraignment, the attorney general's office released an unnervingly detailed twenty-three-page report. In the presentment, the prosecutor itemized the reasons why a statewide grand jury recommended charges of twenty-one felonies and nineteen misdemeanors against Sandusky. Citing the sworn accounts of young men who said they had been sexually assaulted by Sandusky, the report outlined how Sandusky had drawn the vulnerable boys into personal relationships with expensive gifts, clothing, and money and taken them to Penn State and National Football League games. Given the heinous nature of the charges, authorities had taken great pains to protect the identities of the accusers. In the presentment, the boys were referred to by number, from "Victim 1" through "Victim 8." Most damning was the allegation that Sandusky had run his charity to target his prey. "It was within The Second Mile program that Sandusky found his victims," the presentment said. "Through The Second Mile, Sandusky had access to hundreds of boys, many of whom were vulnerable due to their social situations."

Each young man who had opened up when an investigator knocked on his door believed he was the only one who had been abused by Sandusky. Only when the young men read the presentment did they realize that what had happened to them had happened to others. The lawyer for one of the young men, identified as Victim 6, would later seemingly speak for all of them when he described his client's reaction to the presentment: "He cried. He didn't cry for what happened to him. He cried for the others." The pattern of Sandusky's activities had finally come to light.

The document also cited an "uncooperative atmosphere" at Penn State during the investigation. The last sentence, placed in parentheses, pointed out that Sandusky was presumed innocent until proven guilty. Little attention, if any, was paid to that detail.

When the news story broke, the shockwaves were unstoppable. *Jerry Sandusky, known as a male Mother Theresa, charged as a sexual predator assaulting boys in his charity? Rapes of boys in the showers of the Penn State football locker room? Penn State officials covering it up charged with perjury? Penn State, the hallowed domain of the deified Joe Paterno and his "Success with Honor," besmirched by scandal?*

What set this story apart from other media firestorms was how it crossed from news shows to the sports channels. Every channel seemed to be playing a continuous loop of Sandusky entering the district court in handcuffs. Newspapers posted accounts on their websites hours before the story could get into their Sunday editions. The social networks also spread the story. Smartphones programmed to receive updates on Penn State football were beeping with alerts. It was the kind of story nobody wanted to hear but everyone wanted to share.

The Penn State administration knew the arrests were coming. The investigation of Sandusky had first been reported in March by the Harrisburg *Patriot-News,* even though the story then didn't gain much traction beyond central Pennsylvania. Starting in May the thirty-two members of the Penn State board of trustees were briefed about the investigation. Besides Paterno, Curley, Schultz, and Spanier, as many as twenty other university personnel had been called to testify before the grand jury. Some were asked to describe Sandusky's actions, others to explain why they didn't take definitive action after they twice heard specific accusations against him dating back to 1998. Still, when the arrests came, the Penn State administration seemed to be caught off guard.

Inside the president's office in Old Main, Spanier spent hours trying to figure out what to say to the public, his staff, and everyone in the athletic program. He wrote and rewrote his statement as a few of his trusted aides peeked over his shoulder. After he had gone over it ten times or so, he called a meeting for four o'clock with his staff. He told them there was virtually nothing he could say about the charges against Sandusky, other than that he felt pain for the young men. As for Curley and Schultz, he told his staff one option would be to take a strict public relations stand, distancing the university and himself from them. Then he read them the statement he had crafted, which voiced unconditional support for both men. He told his staff that Curley and Schultz had believed Sandusky's actions were inappropriate horseplay, not sexual molestation. Therefore the right thing for him to do was to support them, even if that approach cost him his job. Spanier said he would rather lose his job and live with the belief that he had done what he thought was right than refuse to support two loyal employees. In what Spanier considered a "teachable moment," he told his staff that under similar circumstances, he would remain loyal to all of them too.

The statement Spanier eventually released to the media was this: "The allegations about a former coach are troubling, and it is appropriate that they be investigated thoroughly. Protecting children requires the utmost vigilance. I have known and worked daily with Tim and Gary for more than sixteen years. I have complete confidence in how they have handled the allegations about a former university employee. Tim Curley and Gary Schultz operate at the highest levels of honesty, integrity and compassion. I am confident the record will show that these charges are groundless and they conducted themselves professionally and appropriately."

Meanwhile a statement was released by the CEO of The Second Mile, John Raykovitz, who had been told by Sandusky three years earlier that he was the target of a molestation probe. "All of us at The Second Mile are shaken," the statement said. "This clearly is a difficult time for Jerry and his family, for all other involved parties, and for The Second Mile. However, The Second Mile clearly understands our highest priority must continue to be the safety and well-being of the children participating in our programs." It concluded with the sentence, "At no time was The Second Mile made aware of the very serious allegations contained in the grand jury report," distinctly ignoring the fact that top officials of The Second Mile had been told about the troubling 1998 and 2002 Sandusky incidents shortly after they were reported. .

On Sunday, with no officials speaking publicly, media outlets sharpened their focus on the unfolding scandal by delving into the twenty-three-page grand jury report. Some reporters had already made their way to the campus, while assignment editors for national press organizations dispatched cameras, crews, and satellite trucks to State College. Once the media beast had found this juicy scandal, its appetite was insatiable.

At his home on McKee Street, Joe Paterno was besieged with media requests for comments. He issued a brief statement: "If true, the nature and amount of charges made are very shocking to me and all Penn Staters. . . . The fact that someone we thought we knew might have harmed young people to this extent is deeply troubling. If this is true, we were all fooled, along with scores of professionals trained in such things, and we grieve for the victims and their families. They are in our prayers."

Paterno also tried to explain his own role in the case laid out by prosecutors. In 2002, when he was told that a naked Sandusky was spotted in the football showers with a boy, Paterno said, he did what the law required: he reported it up the Penn State chain of command. In his statement he said, "As my grand jury testimony stated, I was informed in 2002 by an assistant coach that he had witnessed an incident in the shower of our locker room facility. It was obvious the witness was distraught over what he saw, but he at no time related to me the very specific actions contained in the grand jury report. . . . I understand that people are upset and angry, but let's be fair and let the legal process unfold. In the meantime I would ask all Penn Staters to continue to trust in what that name represents, continue to pursue their lives every day with high ideals and not let these events shake their beliefs in who they are."

The Penn State Board of Trustees, sensing the gravity of the rapidly unfolding developments, held the first of several emergency meetings Sunday night, most members attending by conference call. Sandusky was banned from campus altogether. Curley was placed on administrative leave. Schultz, who had retired from the university in 2009 and emerged from retirement on an as-needed basis, returned to retirement. The university announced it would be paying the legal fees for Curley and Schultz.

Students awoke Monday morning to find the streets lined with TV satellite trucks. News organizations from ABC to CNN to ESPN were plumbing Penn State for details. However, the big news event was in Harrisburg. The attorney general's office held its news conference on its investigation and the arrests. Prosecutors emphasized that Paterno had followed the letter of the law by reporting what he knew to his nominal superiors, but the investigation was continuing.

State Police Commissioner Frank Noonan, who had seen combat as a Marine Corps officer in Vietnam, talked about the fallout just beginning to damage the university. Of McQueary's allegations, the state's top cop said, "I don't think I've ever been associated with a case with this type of eyewitness identification of sex acts taking place where the police weren't called." Noonan emphasized that all citizens, including big-name football coaches, have a moral responsibility to protect children. "This is not a case about football. It's not a case about universities. It's a case about children who have had their innocence stolen from them and a culture that did nothing to stop it or prevent it from happening to others."

Jennifer Storm, the executive director of the Victim/Witness Assistance Program in Harrisburg, who herself was a Penn State alumna, used a meeting with the media to urge other young men who might be out there to come for counseling. Storm is the author of three books about the emotional demons that have plagued her since she was raped at the age of twelve. "The totality of the charges made the biggest impact," she said in a later interview. "It's easy to refute one or two people, but the number of those talking about sexual abuse continued to build. From the time I read the presentment, it was black and white. I was physically sick to my stomach. The Penn State administration knew about it and failed to do anything except to protect themselves and their institution. They created a grooming playground. But I also sobbed hysterically for all the alumni and all those who bleed Blue and White. They didn't ask for any of this."

Meanwhile Curley and Schultz surrendered and were arraigned before Magisterial District Judge Marsha Stewart. Bail was set at $75,000 each, which they posted before they were released. Caroline Roberto, the attorney representing Curley, said the charge of failing to report Sandusky under the Child Protective Services Law was a "summary offense" that was the legal equivalent of a traffic ticket. "It's unconscionable that the attorney general would level such a weak case against a man of integrity like Tim Curley," she said. "A perjury charge is a red flag that the charges against him are weak. . . . Tim Curley is innocent of all charges against him. We will vigorously challenge the charges in court, and we are confident he will be exonerated."

At the Atherton Street offices of The Second Mile in State College, messages intended for the media were taped to the locked front door. One statement read, "We do not feel an interview would be appropriate, since this matter involves a criminal investigation, and we do not want to do anything that might interfere with law enforcement officials or the legal process."

On Tuesday, November 8, the *Patriot-News* ran an editorial that took up the entire front page. In type normally reserved for headlines, the editorial declared, "There are obligations we all have to uphold the law. There are then the obligations we all have to do what is right." The *Daily Collegian,* a student-run newspaper on the Penn State campus, also editorialized, "The moral failure of every single person involved is appalling. No one did anything more than try to sweep this problem off-campus. . . . The university has brought shame upon itself."

No Penn State official had yet faced the media since Sandusky's arrest. Paterno was being blasted in the media and throughout the nation because he passed the damning allegations against Sandusky by McQueary off to Curley and did nothing after it was hushed up without a formal investigation. Some were calling for his scalp. Behind the scenes, Graham Spanier asked the board to give him the authority to be the crisis manager and the voice of the university, even though there was mounting outrage over his support of Curley and Schultz. Spanier also argued against the sentiment of a few board members to cancel the upcoming Nebraska game, and possibly the rest of the football season. Having urged the trustees to spare Paterno's job, Spanier also asked for a vote of confidence that would show a united front. The trustees refused all of Spanier's requests.

Throughout his career Joe Paterno held weekly meetings with the media on Tuesdays, so on November 8, the Tuesday following Sandusky's arrest, the media horde, larger than ever, assembled in the interview room at Beaver Stadium. Less than an hour before the news conference was to start, Spanier canceled it. Paterno walked past the assembled reporters while making his way to the regularly scheduled football practice. "I know you guys have a lot of questions," he remarked. "I was hoping I could answer them today. We'll try to do it as soon as we can."

The board of trustees issued its own statement, saying it was outraged by the horrifying details laid out by prosecutors. It said a special committee had been appointed to ensure that a scandal like the one unfolding would never happen at Penn State again. The board was acknowledging that the university had lost its most precious asset: trust. The statement continued, "We cannot begin to express the combination of sorrow and anger that we feel. . . . We are dedicated to protecting those who are placed in our care. We promise you that we are committed to restoring public trust in the university."

As evening fell, some students gathered at Old Main, home to the university's administrative offices. Others, agitated by all the media attention, congregated at various spots on campus and in State College. Some maintained a vigil at the Paterno house on McKee Street. Sue Paterno came to the door and blew a kiss to the well-wishers. Her son Scott asked the students to pray for the victims, saying, "No matter how this works out, there is a horrible story involving a lot of kids getting hurt. . . . Let's remember to show support for the victims first." The students in the yard formed a circle of unity and observed a minute of silence.

A short time later Paterno came to the window to thank his supporters. "I feel sorry for the victims," he said. "We are Penn State. We are family. . . . I lived for this place. I've lived for people like you guys and girls. It's hard for me to say how much this means. Beat Nebraska!"

WEDNESDAY, NOVEMBER 9, WAS A day of inevitability for Joe Paterno. For decades he had talked about stepping down as coach but had always found a reason to stay on. Now, in the final year of his latest contract, with an uproar too loud to control, Paterno attempted to leave on his own terms. He announced his resignation after forty-six years as head coach and sixty-one seasons at Penn State. He was the most acclaimed coach in the history of college football. He had piled up more victories, more winning seasons, and more bowl victories than any other coach. He had won two National Championships, fielded five undefeated teams, and won three Big Ten championships. He had been named "Coach of the Year" five times by the American Football Coaches Association, and he had stayed with one school longer than had any other coach. Some 350 of his players had played professionally in the National Football League, thirty-three of them first-round draft choices. JoePa had produced seventy-eight first-team All-Americans and coached one Heisman Trophy winner. What's more, under his watch Penn State had forty-seven Academic All-Americans, including sixteen honored as scholar-athletes by the National Football Foundation. During his time at Penn State twelve different men had occupied the White House, starting with Harry Truman in 1950. JoePa was the face of Penn State, the central figure in its money-raising machine. In the college bookstore life-size figures of Paterno, called "Stand-up Joes," were sold along with all manner of items bearing his likeness. Now his reign was coming to an end.

Paterno intended to coach through the rest of the season, three more regular season games. By so doing he could break Amos Alonzo Stagg's mark for most games coached in a career. The Nittany Lions were still in contention for the Big Ten championship, and they would surely be invited to a bowl game. At that point there could be a grand farewell for the beloved coach.

"I am absolutely devastated by the developments in this case. I grieve for the children and their families, and I pray for their comfort and relief," Paterno said in a statement. "At this moment, the board of trustees should not spend a single minute discussing my status. They have far more important matters to address. I want to make this as easy for them as I possibly can. This is a tragedy. It is one of the great sorrows of my life. With the benefit of hindsight, I wish I had done more. My goals are to keep my commitments to my players and staff and to finish the season with dignity and determination. And then I will spend the rest of my life doing everything I can to help this university."

For several days, however, the board of trustees had been contemplating what to do about Paterno and his future. It considered Paterno's ongoing status important enough to address later that day.

At the Lasch Building, where the Nittany Lions had gathered for practice, Paterno met privately for ten minutes with his team to tell them of his decision to leave his coaching post. He broke down as he spoke the words. Players witnessed their coach crying for the first time in sixty-one years. After the emotional announcement, Paterno watched practice from his golf cart before heading home. He had no idea that this Wednesday practice would be his final act as a coach.

Meanwhile an artist named Michael Pilato was making alterations to his massive mural *Inspiration,* which adorns the side of a building half a block long on Heister Street near the campus bookstore. He had been working on the mural for ten years, and it features many of the personalities from Penn State and State College, including Jerry Sandusky. The mother of one of Sandusky's accusers had emailed him that morning to suggest that he remove Sandusky's image, and now Pilato climbed a ladder with paintbrush in hand. He proceeded to paint Sandusky out, telling reporters, "It saddens me to do this. He fooled me like he fooled everyone." Painting over the damage wrought by Sandusky would not be that easy. The artist painted a blue ribbon, the symbol used in campaigns against child abuse, on the mural where Sandusky had been portrayed sitting in a chair. He also painted a blue ribbon on the shirt of a smiling Joe Paterno, the central figure of the grand masterpiece.

By the time the Penn State Board of Trustees met in another emergency session that Wednesday night, its vice chairman, John Surma, chief executive officer of U.S. Steel, had been chosen to speak for the university in place of Spanier. Instead of following the university president's suggestions on crisis management, the board chose to retain the services of a national public relations firm, Ketchum, based in New York City. The sixteen-year president realized his time had come. He stepped down, effective immediately. Joe Paterno was not even allowed to dictate the terms of his retirement, and was fired on the spot, after six decades of unflinching devoted service.

Word that the board of trustees had taken action against JoePa reached the Paterno household in a note delivered by Fran Ganter, associate athletic director for football, at 10:15 P.M. The note carried a telephone number, nothing more. There was urgency. The board had scheduled a press conference at the Penn Stater Hotel for 10:30 that evening, fifteen minutes away. According to reports, Paterno called the phone number and talked with Surma, who gave him the news of his dismissal. He hung up without saying a word.

In addressing the media that night, Surma said, "We thought that because of the difficulties that engulfed our university—and they are great—it was necessary for us to make a change in the leadership and set a course for a new direction. The university is much larger than its athletic programs."

About twenty minutes after he was given the axe, Joe Paterno came to his front door to address a group of about forty students who had gathered to support him. With his wife at his side, Paterno said, "Right now, I'm not the coach, and I have to get used to that. I didn't think it was going to happen this way."

The news conference was televised in the student union. Some students reacted angrily to what had happened to Paterno, shouting, "Fuck Graham Spanier. Fuck Sandusky." Facebook posts called for immediate demonstrations. About 2,000 students funneled their way into town through Beaver Canyon, the core of the student apartment area that stretches between McAllister and Garner Streets, leading to Beaver Avenue. They were chanting, "Fuck the trustees! Fuck the media!" and setting off fireworks. On College Avenue nearby, rioting students in range of surveillance cameras tore down a lamppost and street signs. They also flipped over the news truck of WTAJ-TV, a CBS affiliate from Altoona. The damage that night was estimated to be in the range of $200,000. State College police, reinforced by state troopers on horseback, donned riot gear and had tear gas at the ready in case the demonstrations got further out of hand.

Outside Old Main some students voiced quieter messages. One held a sign that said, "Kids before Football." Another's placard read, "Paterno's Not a Victim."

A week or so before Sandusky's arrest, Governor Tom Corbett had alerted Penn State officials that he would attend the regularly scheduled meeting of the board of trustees on November 10. One of the duties of the governor is to serve on the board that has oversight of the university. Corbett had also been the state's attorney general when the investigation into Sandusky had begun three years earlier. While there is no evidence to indicate that the governor had inside information that the arrests of Sandusky, Curly, and Schultz were coming down, his timing was impeccable: he was present to hold a news conference on Thursday, November 10. He used the occasion to express his disappointment in Joe Paterno and Graham Spanier and to support the board's decision made the night before to fire Paterno and accept Spanier's resignation. "Their actions cause me to not have confidence in their ability to lead. . . . When it comes to the safety of children, there can be no margin for error, no hesitation to act," Corbett said.

Just prior to the vote on the fate of Spanier and Paterno, Corbett said, he told the other trustees, "We must remember that ten-year-old child and those other children." The governor applauded the Penn State student leaders for showing solidarity with the young men. As for the students who flipped over the TV truck and lashed out with destructive acts, Corbett called them "knuckleheads."

The *Daily Collegian* published an editorial: "Wednesday night was an embarrassment for Penn State. . . . The way the students reacted set our university two steps back."

On Thursday, November 10, an interim head football coach was introduced. Tom Bradley, a Johnstown native who played football as a defensive back under Paterno and was captain of the special teams unit, was the man. As a player, he was given the nickname "Scrap" because he was undersized but full of fight. Bradley had been a member of the coaching staff for thirty-three years. He had succeeded Sandusky as defensive coordinator in 1999, and he was often mentioned as Paterno's heir-apparent.

Ordinarily the coach would be answering questions about the upcoming game with Nebraska. But when Bradley held his first news conference, in the same Beaver Stadium media room where JoePa sparred with reporters, football questions took a backseat. "Coach Paterno has meant more to me than anybody except my father. Coach Paterno will go down in history as one of the greatest men. . . . I'm proud to say I worked for him," Bradley said. As for the job ahead, Bradley was optimistic. "We are obviously in a very unprecedented situation," he said. "I just have to find a way to restore the confidence and to start a healing process with everybody." It was noted that Mike McQueary would be on the sidelines for Saturday's game. Bradley said it was the university's decision.

On Friday, November 11, the university reversed itself and said Assistant Coach Mike McQueary would not be on the sidelines for Saturday's game. McQueary was put on indefinite administrative leave with full pay after a number of threats on his life were received.

Rodney Erickson, a long-time Spanier underling who had worked in several administrative jobs at Penn State, was sworn in as Penn State's interim president. In his first address to the public he said, "Healing cannot occur until we understand how responsibilities to these children failed and how we can prevent such tragedies in the future." He also promised a new era of openness and transparency in conducting school business. "Never again should anyone at Penn State—regardless of their position—feel scared to do the right thing."

After a week that had exhausted the emotions of just about everyone, calm descended on campus Friday evening. Jessica Sever, a senior majoring in public relations, helped organize a candlelight vigil to show support for the boys mentioned in the investigation. The vigil was held on the lawn in front of Old Main, where two nights earlier angry students had gathered before going on a destructive tear in State College. About 10,000 students attended the vigil—five times more than the number who rioted. At ten o'clock, when the bells in the Old Main tower rang, a moment of silence was observed for the alleged victims. Cheerleaders, who normally would be getting the student body pumped up for the big game against Nebraska, handed out blue placards that said "Stop Child Abuse" instead.

A funereal mood hung over the event. Survivors of sex abuse took the microphone. One said, "These allegations of abuse are horrifying. The people who need our support the most are being overlooked by the entire frenzy." Sandusky's accusers, the eight young men who had told their stories to investigators, received recognition in a solemn roll call, identified individually as Victim 1, Victim 2, and so on.

One speaker at the vigil was LaVar Arrington, a star linebacker on Sandusky's final team, who had been chosen in 2000 with the second overall pick of the NFL draft by the Washington Redskins. "The biggest crime we can commit is to leave here and forget what happened," Arrington told the crowd.

Meanwhile some Penn State alumni set up a fund independent of anything the university was doing. It was designed to raise $500,000 for the victims, roughly a dollar for each of the Penn State alums scattered around the country. The idea started with Jerry and Jaime Needel of Hoboken, New Jersey. Partly out of the shame they felt for what happened and the way some students had reacted on campus, the couple launched a website, proudtobeapennstater.com, with proceeds to be donated to the Rape, Abuse and Incest National Network. By Friday night more than $200,000 had already been pledged. Said Jerry Needel on the website, "We needed to get our pride back. I felt betrayed, and really disgusted. We want to bring attention back where it belongs, with the victims of abuse."

SATURDAY, NOVEMBER 12, DAWNED CLEAR and crisp over a campus that had a cloud hanging over it. Nebraska was in town for the final home game of the season. A bomb squad was called in to do a sweep of Beaver Stadium after a threat had been phoned in, but nothing was found. Nonetheless security was ramped up, and police in riot gear patrolled the outside of the stadium on horseback.

At the Paterno house at the end of McKee Street, white envelopes overflowed from the mailbox even as a mail carrier approached with a bin overloaded with more messages of support. One letter was different from all the others. It was hand-delivered by Jay Paterno, son of the fired coach and a member of the Penn State coaching staff. Jay told his parents not to open it until he had left for the game. He knew he would be too emotional otherwise. The letter, in part, addressed a son's love for his father: "You and I through my life haven't always seen eye-to-eye. But, generally, that's because I had to grow up to catch up and make eye contact with you."

Traffic was bumper-to-bumper coming into State College, just as it always was when Penn State played. In the parking lots, attendants collected $40 for each car and $80 for each recreational vehicle seeking a space. JoePa still had a presence in the form of life-size cutouts set up at tailgate parties. Footballs filled the air and food was served, but some regulars noted a pall that felt like a collective death. Penn State was wrestling for its soul.

Outside Beaver Stadium fans left flowers and messages at the Paterno statue. Ten students had camped out at Paternoville the night before, each with a letter painted on his bare chest. Instead of hyping the Nittany Lions, the letters spelled out "FOR THE KIDS." Face-painting was still in vogue, only this time the blue ribbon symbolizing child abuse prevention adorned cheeks. Some fans held up signs that said "JoePa Got Screwed" and "Screw the Media." One student held up a handmade placard reading, "To the Victims: I Apologize for Penn State."

At the Lasch Building, Penn State players donned their football uniforms and boarded the four blue buses for the one-mile ride to Beaver Stadium. The only reserved seat on any of the buses was the front right seat on the first bus. Joe Paterno always sat there, smiling and waving from the window to the crowds lining the streets. On this day, for the first time, that seat was empty.

Before a home game Penn State players always entered through a tunnel and exploded onto the field. This time they walked out solemnly, arm-in-arm, four at a time, captains in front. Over three hundred former Penn State players were invited to stand on the sidelines for emotional support.

Prior to kickoff, members of both teams moved to the center of the field to join hands and kneel in prayer during a moment of silence. Penn State's interim coach Tom Bradley sought out his counterpart, Nebraska's Bo Pelini, to pray with him. A culture of silence had compounded the issues confronting Penn State, but the silence of 107,000 fans was more deafening than the noise normally generated.

On the field a prayer was offered by Nebraska's running back coach Ron Brown, who had been approached by the Penn State chapter of Athletes in Action to say some appropriate words. Brown was a graduate of Brown University, where Paterno had played football six decades earlier. His words weren't broadcast to the crowd, but the gist of what he said was picked up by TV microphones. Inside the circle of players, Brown walked back and forth like a preacher on the move as he prayed, "Lord, we know that we don't have control of all the events that took place this week, but we do know that you are bigger than it all. Father, God, there are a lot of little boys around the country today who are watching this game, and they're trying to figure out what the definition of manhood is all about. I pray that this game would be a training ground of what manhood looks like. That we would compete with fierce intensity, with the honor and gifts and talent that you've given us. May the truth be known, may justice be known, may you protect the victims." Addressing the players, he continued, "Would you say grace and forgiveness for the lives of all of those involved? Now give us a great game, a game that honors you, and in Jesus' name, we pray. Amen."

The start of the game restored a sense of normalcy. It had been a week since Sandusky's arrest, and two weeks since Paterno left the stadium not knowing it was his final game. The Nebraska game was the first played without Paterno on staff since November 19, 1949, when Penn State lost to Pittsburgh 19–0. Today Penn State's first play was a run up the middle, a subtle tribute to the style of football Paterno had installed at the school when he became the head coach in 1966. In a video shown on the electronic scoreboard during a break in the first quarter, Rodney Erickson, the school's interim president, said, "This has been one of the saddest weeks in the history of Penn State and my heart goes out to those who have been victimized. I share your anger and sorrow. Although we can't go back to business as usual, our university must move forward. We are a community."

In the second quarter Nebraska jumped to a 17–0 lead as Penn State seemed out of rhythm. But starting midpoint in the third quarter, the Nittany Lions were fighting back. They scored a couple of touchdowns and had two possessions that could have either tied the game or put them ahead. However, it was not to be. Nebraska held on to eke out a 17–14 win. Tom Bradley lost in his coaching debut, but he felt a higher purpose had been served. "I felt today, just maybe, the healing process started to begin," he said.

To play the game at all had been a hot topic on campus. There had been strong sentiment to forfeit, in light of the monumental situation unfolding. Penn State's interim president defended his decision to play the game,

saying, "I felt this was a time to play, but also was time we could recognize
and bring national focus to the problem of sexual abuse. Our players and
everyone involved, the way they conducted themselves today, proved that
this was the right decision. This was the way to do it."

On the opposing side, Bo Pelini was thankful for more than just a victory. "I'll be honest with you. Before the game, I didn't think it should have
been played for a lot of different reasons," he said in his postgame remarks.
"I don't know the specifics of the situation, and I'm not judging anybody.
But the fact is, kids were hurt. And that's a lot bigger than football. . . . I
think both teams coming together was the right thing to do and hopefully
that in itself made a statement."

Joe Paterno's son Jay, an assistant coach at Penn State for seventeen
seasons, usually sat in the coaches' box high above the field, but was invited
to coach against Nebraska from the sidelines. He handled his duties wearing the style of black shoes his father preferred and the jacket his dad had
worn during the game in which he broke Bear Bryant's record for career victories. After the game Jay told reporters, "The world's kind of turned upside
down." Then he walked to his parents' house, where his mother always
served a postgame dinner to forty or so family members and special guests.

Before, during, and after the Penn State-Nebraska showdown, Joe's
supporters mingled outside the Paterno home. A cop kept them off the
lawn and allowed only family members and guests to approach the front
door. Many people left signs or notes for JoePa. Cathy Taylor of Roanoke,
Virginia, left this sign: "Despite everything, someone like you deserved to
be treated with more dignity and respect than a phone call to your home.
And for that, we are sorry. Thanks. Enjoy your retirement. You've earned it."

In the gloaming, the descending autumn sun created long shadows
through the leafless trees in Sunset Park, a public space adjacent to the
Paterno home. Sue Paterno emerged from the house and spoke briefly to
those who were still lingering on the sidewalk. She told them, "I've always
felt Penn State was a family. We will be again. We'll be back. We're not
going anywhere."

• • •

FALLOUT EXTENDED BEYOND THE PENN State campus. On Sunday, November 13, The Second Mile announced that it had accepted the resignation of John Raykovitz, a practicing psychologist who had run the organization for twenty-eight years. His wife, the organization's executive vice president, Katherine Genovese, tendered her resignation as well. The Second Mile said it was going to conduct an internal investigation to assess its policies and make recommendations regarding its future. It also said it had hired a new legal firm.

Meanwhile Governor Corbett made the rounds on the Sunday morning TV news shows. On *Fox News Sunday* he said that Paterno had met his legal obligation in the Sandusky scandal but didn't go as far as he should have: "When you don't follow through, when you don't continue on to make sure that actions are taken, then I lose confidence in your ability to lead. That would be the case here."

Because Penn State receives federal money for research, the U.S. Department of Education entered the case to determine if there had been any violations of the Clery Act, a federal law that mandates reporting of campus crime. The Act was named for a Lehigh University student who had been raped and murdered in 1986. "If it turns out that some people at the school knew of the abuse and did nothing or covered it up, that makes it even worse," Education Secretary Arne Duncan said.

Among the sports analysts later weighing in on the breaking story was Matt Millen, a former Penn Stater who had played defense under Sandusky and who had been an executive with the Detroit Lions after a career in the National Football League. Now a football analyst on ESPN, Millen said in a voice cracking with emotion, "I get mad. . . . If we can't protect our kids we, as a society, are pathetic." Speaking about the events engulfing his alma mater, Millen added, "A horror picture screen writer couldn't write this bad of a script."

On Monday, November 14, during the annual meeting of Catholic bishops in Baltimore, Archbishop Timothy Dolan of New York responded to a question about the Penn State scandal by saying, "Whenever this painful issue comes into public view again, as it has sadly recently with Penn State, it reopens a wound in the church. We once again hang our heads in shame as we recall with contrition those who have been suffering. . . . One of the things we learned the hard way, and Lord knows we earned our Ph.D. in the school of hard knocks on this one, is that education in this area is extraordinarily efficacious."

The National Football Foundation announced it was withdrawing the award it had been planning to bestow on Tim Curley, its John F. Toner Award, presented annually to the athletic director who has shown "outstanding dedication to college athletics and particularly college football."

Pennsylvania's two U.S. senators, Bob Casey and Pat Toomey, announced that they had rescinded their support of Paterno for the Presidential Medal of Freedom, the nation's highest civilian award. Casey, a Democrat, and Toomey, a Republican, had nominated Paterno for the award in September in a letter to President Obama.

The Big Ten Conference announced that it was removing Paterno's name from its championship trophy. In explanation Commissioner Jim Delaney said, "The trophy and its namesake are intended to be celebratory and inspirational, not controversial." The removal of Paterno's name brought a sense of sad finality to Marino Parascenzo, a retired sports writer with the *Pittsburgh Post-Gazette* who had covered Penn State football. "I told my wife that it was like the changing of the dynasties in ancient Egypt," he said. "The new pharaoh would deface the monuments and erase the names of the old pharaoh, as if to show he never existed. Taking Joe's name off that trophy was like taking an eraser to his legacy. It was the ultimate disgrace."

On the Penn State campus, Mount Nittany stood undisturbed. But the festive culture of Happy Valley and Penn State football had crumbled. Joe Paterno and his Grand Experiment were over. But his legacy and demand for personal excellence, as demonstrated in so many of his players, will remain for generations.

CHAPTER ELEVEN

INSULARITY AND ISOLATION

Penn State had a way of doing things in isolation. Nobody had to construct a symbolic Great Wall to separate Happy Valley from the outside world; nature built its own version in the form of Mount Nittany. The myth and folklore of Penn State, along with the insular thinking that went into the university's operations, did the rest.

Nittany is an Algonquin word that means "single mountain." The name was given to the geographic formation that sits at the southern end of two ridgelines of the Appalachian Mountains and rises one thousand feet above a verdant valley in central Pennsylvania. Various legends exist to explain how a formation of quartzite, shale, and sandstone become a mountain. In one popular story a young Native American woman named Nitta-nee taught the valley's inhabitants how to build a barrier against a cruel north wind that had destroyed their crops. After she died of a mysterious illness, the people honored her with a burial mound, which the Great Spirit transformed into Mount Nittany. In another story, a woman named Nit-A-Nee built a burial mound to honor her fallen lover, Lion's Paw. This mound of dirt and rock magically rose up to become the mountain overlooking the picturesque Nittany Valley. Both stories share a common ending: the mountain formed a barrier against the ill winds of the outside world, and the inhabitants who lived in its shadow would know only happiness. Thus was born Happy Valley. Unspoken was the reality that barriers are meaningless against inside threats. Insularity has the unintended consequence of locking in potential danger.

Joe Paterno openly embraced insularity, drawing a blue line around his football program. Unlike other big-time college football programs that have media availabilities daily, outsiders, including sports writers, had only limited access to the Penn State football world. Paterno's practices were closed to the media. He had one media availability a week during football season, conducted by conference call, when reporters were allowed to ask one question each. Interviews with players were arranged through the Sports Information Department. Freshmen were not allowed in front of microphones. On game days the Penn State locker room was closed. Writers could get postgame quotes from Paterno in an interview room inside Beaver Stadium, or take a one-mile bus ride to the Lasch Building to ask questions of players, if they were made available.

Paterno was unapologetic about sealing off his world, even though it sometimes resulted in reprimands. Two examples of insular thinking occurred at the 2009 Rose Bowl in Pasadena, California, where Penn State lost to the University of Southern California 38–24. Paterno was under contractual obligation to give a pregame sideline interview to ABC-TV, which had exclusive rights to televise the game, but he failed to show up as promised. His excuse was that because he had undergone hip-replacement surgery five weeks earlier, he had to get to his seat in the press box from where he was going to coach the game and was unavailable on the sidelines. He said he didn't want to put one of his assistant coaches on the spot to give the interview in his place. After the game, sports writers on deadline discovered that the Penn State locker room was off-limits, a violation of bowl policy. To get quotes for their stories, writers had to depend on a Penn State sports information staffer to bring players out of the room so they could be interviewed in a hallway. The officials who ran the Rose Bowl, which paid

$18 million to Penn State for appearing in its televised extravaganza, fined Paterno and Penn State an undisclosed sum for violating its policy of being open to the media.

Paterno spoke about the fines and explained his closed-door policy to a group of New York City writers prior to a Penn State alumni event on April 30, 2009. The event, called "An Evening with Joe," was held at the Plaza, just off Central Park in Manhattan. "I have never had an open locker room. If you let the men in, you have to let the women in. I don't want a whole bunch of women walking around in my locker room. The players take showers, are horsing around," Paterno told the sports writers. "It's our game. It's not your game. I don't mean that in an adversary [sic] way. It's our football team. When we lose, we want to cry a little bit or maybe there's some guy in the corner, griping he didn't get the ball and all of a sudden someone sticks a microphone in your face."

Writers who covered Penn State football said getting information out of State College was like trying to get information out of the Central Intelligence Agency. After the Sandusky scandal broke and Paterno was ignominiously fired, an opinion piece appeared on November 11, 2011, in the *Centre Daily Times*. It was written by Ron Bracken, a retired sports editor who had spent decades covering Paterno and the Nittany Lions. He compared Paterno's tightly controlled access to "Kremlin-like secrecy." "It was understood that if you wanted to be around his program in a professional aspect, you did so at his pleasure and by his rules. And that kind of climate is a Petri dish for what happened in what must now be called the Sandusky Scandal," Bracken wrote. "It's pervasive on the campus from the lowest worker in the Office of the Physical Plant to the corner offices in Old Main. It's all about keeping your mouth shut, doing your job, looking the other way at the various indiscretions and currying favor with those above you in the food chain in order to keep or improve your position."

Bracken added that the attitude at Penn State was to "protect the image at all costs and if the truth has to be whitewashed to hide it, well, break out the buckets and the brushes." His take on the reaction by the Penn State officials who were notified of Sandusky's activities on campus prior to the state investigation was this: "One after another, five adult males dismissed it as inconsequential, doing the bare minimum to even acknowledge it, then passing it up the chain of command and getting back to the business of cultivating and polishing the image. So at the risk of an unsightly blemish on the program, young lives were permanently altered in terrible ways."

One example of the measures Penn State took to guard its secrets was the five-year court fight it waged to keep Paterno's salary from being disclosed, a battle that reached the Pennsylvania Supreme Court. In a lawsuit filed in 2002 the *Patriot-News* of Harrisburg argued that the state's public records law, known as the Pennsylvania Right to Know Act, required Penn State and the State Employees Retirement Board to reveal salaries of top officials at institutions that receive public money and to reveal public records if asked. Penn State received about $450 million a year in state funds. But the university balked and took its case to the state supreme court. The school argued that it should not be bound by the law because disclosure would violate the privacy of the officials whose salaries were the subject of the argument. Justice Cynthia Baldwin recused herself from the case. She was a Penn State graduate and trustee and therefore thought she was too personally involved. She later became the university's general counsel.

In November 2007 the court ruled against Penn State and the salaries were made available. Paterno, the university's chief fundraiser, was the highest paid person at the school. In his final year he was paid more than $1 million, not counting money from contracts with Nike and television deals. In the wacky world of college sports, his salary sat in the bottom half for coaches in the Big Ten Conference and was a fraction of the megadeals in place at other colleges. Still, as a football coach, he made $200,000 more a year than the university president. At the time his salary was made public Paterno told a gathering of sports writers, "It bothers me that people have to know what I make. What difference does it make what I make? I don't know what you guys make."

Another insight into Penn State insularity was its fight to avoid being included in a new Pennsylvania public records law that was approved in 2009. Graham Spanier even made a personal appearance before the legislative committee developing the law. He argued that including Penn State

On August 6, 1999, Penn State head football coach Joe Paterno, right, posed with Jerry Sandusky during the former defensive coordinator's last Penn State Media Day at State College, Pennsylvania. *(AP Photo/Paul Vathis)*

Jerry Sandusky wins the last game in which he serves as defensive coordinator, in a 24-0 shutout over Texas A & M in the December 28, 1999, Alamo Bowl.

(LEFT) Joe Paterno has a word with wide receiver Tony Johnson during a game against Temple in 2003. (*Copyright* Pittsburgh Post-Gazette. *All rights reserved. Reprinted with permission.*)

(RIGHT) Joe Paterno argues with a referee while pointing to the replay on the scoreboard in a game against Iowa in 2004. (*Copyright* Pittsburgh Post-Gazette. *All rights reserved. Reprinted with permission.*)

Penn State fans cheer during a "whiteout" at Beaver Stadium in a game against Ohio State in 2007. (*Copyright* Pittsburgh Post-Gazette. *All rights reserved. Reprinted with permission.*)

Jubilant players carry Joe Paterno off the field after his 400th career win, against Northwestern in 2010. (*Copyright* Pittsburgh Post-Gazette. *All rights reserved. Reprinted with permission.*)

(LEFT) Joe Paterno greets Tamba Hali, a defensive star, who returned to Penn State for graduation ceremonies in 2006. (*Copyright* Pittsburgh Post-Gazette. *All rights reserved. Reprinted with permission.*)

(RIGHT) Joe Paterno addresses the media from his golf cart at a media day in August 2011. (*Copyright* Pittsburgh Post-Gazette. *All rights reserved. Reprinted with permission.*)

Joe Paterno awaits the start of his final football practice on November 8, 2011. He was fired later in the day. *(Copyright* Pittsburgh Post-Gazette. *All rights reserved. Reprinted with permission.)*

Quarterback Matt McGloin is greeted by fans as he enters Beaver Stadium before the game against Nebraska on November 12, 2011. *(Copyright* Pittsburgh Post-Gazette. *All rights reserved. Reprinted with permission.)*

Interim Coach Tom Bradley waves to fans before a game with Nebraska on November 12, 2011.

The Atherton Street main offices of The Second Mile, founded by Jerry Sandusky in 1977. The charity is considering its options, including closing altogether. (*Bill Moushey*)

After Sandusky's second arrest on child molestation charges, this mug shot was taken at the Centre County Correctional Center. *(Centre County Correctional Center)*

(LEFT) Tim Curley's mug shot taken after his arrest on November 6, 2011, on charges of perjury and failing to report child abuse related to the Sandusky case. *(Pennsylvania Attorney General)*

(RIGHT) If Gary Schultz is found guilty of perjury and failure to report child abuse, charges for which he was arrested on November 6, 2011, he could lose a $5 million pension benefit. *(Pennsylvania Attorney General)*

Hundreds of Penn State students rally in support of Penn State head football coach Joe Paterno outside his State College, Pennsylvania, home Tuesday, November 8, 2011, after he announced he would step down as coach at the end of the 2011 season. *(Photograph by Andy Colwell)*

Penn State freshman Jordan Barr, center, of Lancaster, holds a sign as he and hundreds of Penn State students gather outside Paterno's State College, Pennsylvania, home Tuesday, November 8, 2011. *(Photograph by Andy Colwell)*

Joe Paterno, former Penn State football coach, speaks to gathered students and media outside his home in State College, Pennsylvania, Tuesday, November 8, 2011, in direct response to his announcement earlier in the day that he would step down as coach at the end of the 2011 season. *(Photograph by Andy Colwell)*

Joe Paterno stands at the window of his home to acknowledge support of students rallying in his front yard.

Students gathered by the thousands along Beaver Avenue in downtown State College late Tuesday, November 8, 2011, to show their support for Joe Paterno. (*Photograph by Andy Colwell*)

Rioters flip over a news van after word that Joe Paterno was fired leaks out across State College, Pennsylvania. (*Copyright* Pittsburgh Post-Gazette. *All rights reserved. Reprinted with permission.*)

After organizing a protest, Penn State students converge on campus and in downtown State College, Pennsylvania, on Tuesday, November 8, 2011, to support Joe Paterno. (*Photograph by Andy Colwell*)

The Joe Paterno cardboard cutout makes an appearance during a rally against JoPa's firing.

Thousands gather outside Penn State's Old Main administration building on Friday, November 11, 2011, during a Penn State student-organized candlelight vigil to show student support for victims of child sexual abuse. The event drew as many as 10,000, according to unofficial police estimates. *(Photograph by Andy Colwell)*

Penn State student Adam Adamietz sings during the candlelight vigil in support of victims of child sexual abuse. *(Photograph by Andy Colwell)*

Candles held aloft by Penn State students join thousands of others outside the Old Main administration building. *(Photograph by Andy Colwell)*

Jerry Sandusky, with his wife, Dottie, as he enters the Centre County Courthouse in Bellefonte, Pennsylvania, on the day of his preliminary hearing on child abuse charges. Once inside, he waives his right to the hearing. *(Copyright* Pittsburgh Post-Gazette. *All rights reserved.*

Satellite trucks become a fixture at Penn State after the November 2011 charges were filed against Jerry Sandusky and two others. *(Bill Moushey)*

Reporters jam the front yard of the Centre County Courthouse in the aftermath of the waived preliminary hearing on December 13, 2011. *(Copyright* Pittsburgh Post-Gazette. *All rights reserved. Reprinted with permission.)*

Joe Paterno uses a cane entering Beaver Stadium for a 2008 game against Indiana prior to hip surgery. That was the beginning of a series of health issues for the longtime coach. *(Copyright Pittsburgh Post-Gazette. All rights reserved. Reprinted with permission.)*

On the day Joe Paterno is laid to rest, fans flock to the statue commemorating his life outside Penn State's Beaver Stadium. *(Bill Moushey)*

A metallic-blue hearse takes Joe Paterno on his last ride past Beaver Stadium on the day of his burial. *(Bill Moushey)*

Mike McQueary is consoled by Christine Johnson, wife of Penn State assistant coach Larry Johnson.

Twenty-seven thousand people pay tribute to Joe Paterno at the Pasquerilla Spiritual Center on the Penn State University campus.

Artist Michael Pilato paints
over a likeness of Jerry
Sandusky on a mural on
the wall of the Penn State
bookstore depicting famous
people from Happy Valley.
(Copyright Pittsburgh Post-Gazette.
All rights reserved. Reprinted with
permission.)

A halo now adorns the
painting of Joe Paterno on
the mural wall of the campus
bookstore in State College,
Pennsylvania. *(Bill Moushey)*

in the law would affect fundraising from private individuals and companies that would not want their contributions to be made public. He said the university's costs would grow and employee morale would be destroyed if the university was forced to abide by the rules of transparency. Spanier also said that inclusion in a public records law would compromise the $100 million the school receives in grants and contracts from industry each year. Public notification would violate the confidentiality of donors, erode privacy rights of individuals, and hinder incentive and merit pay programs because all employees could have access to what others earn. Spanier pointed out if Penn State was included in the public records law, it would also have to reveal information about complimentary tickets to football games, or free bowl trips or other considerations it might have offered legislators.

Despite the fact that most state universities in Pennsylvania are obliged to follow the open records law, Penn State successfully fought to keep itself excluded. In the wake of the Sandusky scandal, a bipartisan group of state legislators was considering an end to the exemptions. State Representative Eugene DePasquale introduced a bill that would require all state and municipal government entities to provide access to records, including all financial documents, campus police reports, contracts, and emails.

The insularity of Penn State and the way it controls its athletic endeavors became the focus of an investigation by the National Collegiate Athletic Association. While Penn State has long enjoyed a reputation as one of only four schools never sanctioned by the regulatory body, after the Sandusky scandal erupted the NCAA announced that it was starting a probe into whether its regulations governing the ethical conduct of a sports program had been compromised. Under a rule regarding "institutional control," which requires member schools to conduct appropriate oversight in order to detect and investigate violations, the NCAA is trying to determine whether the school lived up to its obligations. Failures in that area could cause a range of sanctions, including bans from participating in intercollegiate athletics and bowl games and the loss of athletic scholarships. Along with the NCAA, the Big Ten Conference and the university itself are conducting separate probes to, as the Big Ten said in a written statement, examine "significant concerns as to whether a concentration of power in a single individual or program may have threatened or eroded institutional control of intercollegiate athletics at Penn State."

Transparency was also an issue when the former FBI director Louis Freeh was named to head a nine-member investigating committee looking into the Sandusky scandal, because the school initially refused to disclose how much Freeh's firm is being paid. The university took great pains to declare the probe independent, yet Freeh is the only person associated with the probe who does not have Penn State ties. He is empowered to take the investigation in any direction he deems necessary, but it is the committee who will receive the findings and determine who should be held responsible. Most important, the committee of insiders will decide what, if anything, is made public. Penn State also refused to disclose how much it is paying Ketchum, the public relations firm it hired to control its message about the scandal. Later, the university said it had paid the Freeh group $1.1 million and Ketchum almost $500,000 through the end of 2011.

In the aftermath of Sandusky's indictment, critics of Governor Tom Corbett suggested that politics may have caused the investigation to languish for years.

During a speech before the Pennsylvania Press Club after the indictment was released in November 2011, Corbett said he had been driven by a desire to conduct a thorough investigation, not by politics. "The one thing you do not want to do as a prosecutor is go on one case. You want to show a continued course of action," he was quoted as saying in a transcript of his remarks. If he had filed a set of charges as soon as one credible accusation was established, it could have ruined the entire investigation. "It would be much more difficult to bring charges in other cases because it would be seen by you, by the public, as vindictive."

The governor said he was very careful about mentioning the probe in a political context because he did not want to reveal anything about it, even though a Harrisburg newspaper had reported its existence just two months after he took office in March 2011. "I gave a lot of thought to it on a constant basis," Corbett said. He claimed that only two people in his administration knew any details about the investigation: the commissioner of the Pennsylvania State Police, Frank Noonan, and Corbett's press aide, Kevin Harley.

"Given the nature of the charges against Sandusky, why not simply arrest Sandusky without a grand jury and then proceed to a grand jury to investigate the cover-up?" one reporter asked.

After a long sigh, the governor replied, "The grand jury, as you know, takes quite a while. It doesn't necessarily have to take quite a while, but in cases like this, it does. Once you arrest somebody, particularly if they would have arrested Mr. Sandusky in the very beginning when the case was first brought to us with one witness, now you have times that have to be met [under] rules of criminal procedure. The one thing you do not want to do when you arrest someone, as a prosecutor, is go on one case, at the very beginning, until you have documented everything." In cases of pedophilia, prosecutors should develop more than one incident to show a pattern of action, Corbett said.

Ultimately, the governor said, he was content that the prosecutors made the correct tactical decisions, even if they were being questioned by the media. "You have a right to question them. But these are people that have experience in these fields and they made decisions that I agree with—I made a decision with them when I was there and [current Attorney General] Linda Kelly made the decisions thereafter—this will all play out in the courts."

At a later speech, in Philadelphia, Corbett talked about why the probe took as long as it did. "Could anybody guarantee [Sandusky] wasn't out there touching children? There are no such guarantees, unless he was sitting in jail. But we did what we thought was in the best interests of the investigation in getting a good case put together."

State Police Commissioner Noonan, a Corbett appointee, said there were no politics involved in the investigation. It was true that only one state trooper was assigned to the Sandusky case in the run-up to the governor's election, but Noonan said he added seven investigators in late 2010 because the evidence merited it. Decisions were made out of necessity, not politics: "I can say that I was intimately involved in every decision that was made in this case, and nothing could be further from the truth. Governor Corbett gave us everything we needed to do the investigation and was anxious for it to be concluded as quickly as possible and I had known that because I was involved with it and with him the entire time."

Pennsylvania politics is a lot like its rain: both have some acid in them. The political map of the state is such that a Republican must win big in the conservative middle of the state to offset Democratic strength in the major cities of Philadelphia and Pittsburgh. In his campaign to become attorney general Corbett developed strong support in central Pennsylvania, including from big donors. Many of his supporters there were connected to Penn State and The Second Mile, a fact of life in the region. Penn State, for example, is the largest employer in Centre County, and many of its graduates operate businesses in the region. Large campaign donations to Corbett from those associated with The Second Mile have been documented. According to the National Institute on Money in State Politics, a website that charts contributions to candidates, almost $650,000 in contributions were made over the years to Corbett from donors affiliated with The Second Mile.

State spending was another matter. Corbett, a fiscal conservative, slashed state funds from virtually every area of government to overcome a $500 million budget shortfall. But even though he knew The Second Mile was under the cloud of the Sandusky investigation, he did nothing to stop a $3 million grant to the charity that had been approved by his predecessor. The money was intended to reimburse the charity for expenses incurred in planning for the construction of a 45,000-square-foot education center. Allowing that reimbursement to go forward seemed to run counter to how Corbett handled matters during the biggest criminal investigation of his tenure as attorney general. As the state's top law enforcement officer, he had gone after state legislators suspected of using their public resources and staff workers for private political gain. By the time Corbett left the attorney general's office, that investigation had produced nineteen guilty pleas or convictions of lawmakers and people on their staffs. The investigation had political overtones, and Corbett returned every campaign contribution from anyone who may have been associated with or connected to the investigation.

However, he did not return donations received from Second Mile board members, their businesses, or their families during the initial two years of the Sandusky investigation. The largest of the contributions to Corbett came from the Second Mile board member Lance Shaner, owner of thirty-four hotels in the United States and Italy, including Toftrees Resort and Conference Center in State College. Toftrees runs the hotel where the Penn State football team stays on nights before home games; Joe Paterno didn't like to have his players stay in their dorm rooms then, fearful that they would disrespect curfew. Toftrees was the perfect hideaway, within ten minutes of Beaver Stadium and yet isolated on 1,500 acres, away from campus and the Friday-night Penn State rah-rah. It was later mentioned as the site of at least two allegations of child abuse involving Sandusky. Shaner and a family member contributed $163,275 to the Corbett campaign.

Louie Sheetz, a Penn State grad who sat on the board of The Second Mile, is the executive vice president for marketing at Sheetz Inc., an Altoona-based company that operates a chain of gas stations and convenience stores in Pennsylvania. Sheetz didn't contribute directly to Corbett's campaign chest, but the family-owned company and Sheetz family members contributed a total of $113,350 to Corbett.

Ray Roundtree, regional vice president of finance for Comcast Cable, is also a Second Mile board member. His company and its employees donated another $100,000 to Corbett.

Robert Poole, president of S & A Homes, is chairman of the board of The Second Mile and a long-time Republican donor. He contributed $11,000 and held a fundraiser in January 2010 for Corbett. Poole, an active Penn State alum, also serves as chairman of Penn State's Schreyer Honors College and is a member of the board of visitors for the university's Smeal College of Business.

Corbett said his dual role as the law enforcement officer who started the Sandusky probe and later as the chief executive in control of the state's purse strings complicated his decisions. He thought that rescinding the $3 million grant to The Second Mile or returning contributions from those affiliated with the charity could disclose details of the investigation. "I could not act publicly on [the $3 million grant] without saying certain things that would have possibly compromised the investigation," he told reporters.

Corbett also denied he had any inside information on when Sandusky would be arrested. "I did not know the date that the presentment would come down, or if it would ever come down, because I had pulled myself away from the investigation."

Corbett said he believed the mission of The Second Mile was a good one, and that its programs were beneficial to the vast majority of at-risk kids referred to it. But he withdrew the $3 million state grant shortly after questions were raised about the charity.

Kevin Harley, Corbett's press secretary, did not respond to written questions or otherwise discuss the governor's actions related to the Sandusky probe or the campaign contributions by those affiliated with The Second Mile.

Meanwhile Penn State's new president Rodney Erickson sought to reassure faculty, students, and the public that the university would strive to be more transparent in the future. A native of Wisconsin, Erickson was as much at home farming corn and wheat in the fields outside State College as he was serving in relative obscurity as Penn State's second-highest-ranking administrator. He had arrived at the university in 1977 after earning degrees at the University of Minnesota and the University of Washington. In his thirty-four years at Penn State, he had served as the dean of the graduate school, the vice president for research, and the executive vice president and chief academic officer. Then, under the most challenging conditions imaginable, he took command of the school the night Graham Spanier resigned and Joe Paterno was fired. As the seventeenth president in university history, Erickson promised to rebuild trust and confidence in an institution that had been shaken to its core by a child sex abuse scandal. He pledged to begin a new era of openness to replace a culture of silence that helped foster the conditions that had brought shame to Penn State. He conceded that the insular nature of the school had to change. "Penn State is committed to transparency to the fullest extent possible," Erickson said in his inaugural message, which was addressed to the Penn State community and sent electronically to the school's alumni. "My door will always be open."

Transparency faced challenges from the start, however. Erickson was appointed president without a search, and Pennsylvania's open meetings law, known as the Sunshine Act, may have been violated when a November 9 vote by the thirty-two members of the board of trustees named Erickson president. The law, designed to prevent public agencies from taking action in secret, requires public agencies to give notice of at least twenty-four hours of when and where meetings are to be staged. It also states that individual employees or appointees whose rights could be adversely affected may request that matters be discussed at an open meeting. Paterno was not notified that his job status was on the agenda that night. Although the vote was announced as unanimous, it was not taken in public and therefore could be considered null and void. To make sure it was in compliance with the Sunshine Act, the executive committee of the board of trustees met in a public session weeks later to formally approve its decisions of November 9. In effect, they fired Paterno again.

The Second Mile and Penn State were inextricably linked. The Nittany Lion mascot went to Second Mile golf tournaments and other events wearing a Second Mile T-shirt over his costume. In April 2000 a Jerry Sandusky Dinner and Roast was put on by Penn State Intercollegiate Athletics and sponsored by the credit card giant MBNA as part of the Blue-White Kickoff Weekend. Proceeds went to the Second Mile/Jerry Sandusky Endowment Fund. In 2001 the university sold 40.7 acres in Patton Township to The Second Mile. Of the thirty-seven members on The Second Mile's board of directors, the body that oversees the entire operation, twenty-four are Penn State graduates.

Dottie and Lloyd Huck sat on The Second Mile board. Lloyd, a former president and CEO of Merck & Company, was also a former president of the Penn State University Alumni Association. Board member DrueAnne Schreyer is the daughter of William Schreyer, the former chair and CEO of Merrill Lynch and a former Penn State board of trustees chairman. Katherine Genovese, former vice president of programming at The Second Mile and wife of the deposed CEO John Raykovitz, is an elected member of Penn State's Alumni Association's governing board. State Senator Jake Corman, another Penn State alum, joined the charity's board in 2010.

The Second Mile's annual Celebration of Excellence dinner in Hershey, Pennsylvania, has almost always featured a Penn State presence. The quarterback Matt McGloin was the keynote speaker in 2011. In 2007 the banquet was touted as "A Salute to Linebacker U."

Penn State brought star power to Second Mile events with sports and Hollywood celebrities like the actor Mark Wahlberg and NFL coaches Lou Holtz and Dick Vermeil. Joe Paterno was often at the charity's fundraisers and offered other financial support. Penn State students did internships there, and the football players were always offering their services, working with the young kids in the charity's programs.

After the scandal broke, The Second Mile announced plans to hire outside counsel to conduct an internal investigation into what happened, especially since Penn State leaders had twice informed them about improper conduct between Sandusky and children in the course of a decade. One of the actions The Second Mile is currently considering is shutting its doors.

The child molestation charges against Sandusky were a huge embarrassment for Penn State officials. Having two top university officials, Tim Curley and Gary Schultz, charged with perjury and failure to report abuse of children made the mess that much more upsetting. Prosecutors believed a culture of secrecy had become so pervasive in Happy Valley that officials there were accustomed to handling matters internally.

Frank Noonan, the state police commissioner, said as much in a news conference the Monday after Sandusky's arrest. Noonan criticized Penn State for "doing nothing to stop or prevent harm to the victims in this case." President Graham Spanier had insisted he didn't know about the allegations against Sandusky in 1998 and didn't order a full-scale investigation in 2002, when similar allegations were made, because he was never told they included sexual abuse of children. Nevertheless Noonan blamed insularity and secrecy for allowing such heinous crimes to continue for as long as they did. He admonished Schultz and Curley for having no moral compass and refusing to do anything but cover up repeated allegations that Sandusky was using Penn State facilities to molest children.

Guy Montecalvo, a former Penn State footballer, couldn't believe what he was hearing. The names of the people implicated in this scandal were personal friends. At Penn State he and Tim Curley had been roommates for four years and have enjoyed a friendship for four decades. Guy had introduced Curley to his wife, Melinda Harr. As a roommate, Curley had been a meticulous, committed, and dedicated student who was true blue-and-white.

When Montecalvo's Penn State playing career ended with his fourth knee surgery, he was given a chance to coach as a student and graduate assistant under Joe Paterno. Paterno's guidance helped Montecalvo land a football coaching job at Washington High School, where he built a championship program. Montecalvo later coached football and other sports at Canon-McMillan High School near Pittsburgh before stepping down to serve as athletic director. In 1997 Sandusky had visited the cancer ward at Children's Hospital in Pittsburgh, where Guy's son, Jimmy, was in a fight against the cancer attacking his immune system and white blood cells. Sandusky brought along an authentic Penn State football jersey as a gift, and he stayed for a couple of hours to offer words of encouragement that would lift the young man's spirits. "He just didn't stop in to say hello. He went out of his way to spend some time," said Montecalvo. "But that wasn't atypical of Jerry. He seemed to be one of the most compassionate and caring individuals I ever ran across."

Montecalvo and Sandusky were both inducted into the Pennsylvania Sports Hall of Fame in 1999. Montecalvo had seen Sandusky in early October at Penn State's game against Iowa, when the school marked the twenty-fifth anniversary of winning the 1986 national championship. Now Montecalvo was blindsided by the charges brought against Sandusky and Curley. "I was stunned and shocked. This can't possibly be happening. Jerry Sandusky was a role model as a coach and as a humanitarian. The charges did not compute with the portrait of the man I know. My reaction to the news about Tim Curley was that this is something he would not have done. I do not believe he would lie to a grand jury. I watched the way these guys lived their lives and it helped shape how I've operated as a coach for thirty years. Incomprehensible is not an adjective that adequately described what I was feeling."

The timing of the 1998 investigation and Sandusky's retirement in 1999 remains curious. Sandusky claimed he walked away from a prestigious, lucrative job as one of the best defensive coaches in the country to devote all of his time to the kids at his charity. Besides that, having reached the age of fifty-five, he was eligible for a comfortable retirement package under new regulations just approved by the state. Perhaps the mystery is best phrased in the form of an unanswered question. Why, after twenty-two years of balancing his duties as a coach and the head of a charity, did he leave the football program? Was there something else influencing his decision to leave quietly and remain in State College with all the perks that Penn State still offered him? Or was he really unwilling to cut back on his work at The Second Mile? It is perplexing that after so many successful years as a defensive coordinator, he would not want a head coaching job at another university. His departure, and the way it was handled, baffled many people in the sports world. Paterno didn't even seem that concerned at losing his victory-producing assistant.

By just about every account, Paterno knew everything that was going on at Penn State, especially within his football program. He was so tuned in he even knew when one of his players got an out-of-state traffic ticket. Yet he claimed he didn't know there were police inquiries into his defensive coach's behavior. Why did he give Sandusky, the mastermind behind so many of his victories, a bare minimum salute upon his retirement in 1999? Did the campus police, and later the state police, ever question Paterno about his second-in-command?

Paterno, who has never been accused of any wrongdoing, said he was unaware of the 1998 report by the Penn State campus police, and the case was closed without criminal charges being brought. "You know," Paterno said in January 2012, in an interview with the *Washington Post,* "it wasn't like it was something everybody in the building knew about. Nobody knew about it."

But doubts have been cast by those who contend that Paterno knew everything about the behavior of his players and coaches. Matt Paknis, a graduate assistant on the Penn State coaching staff from February 1987 to August 1988, was sexually abused by a neighbor when he was a boy. Paknis said it was "impossible" that Paterno did not know about the investigation by campus police. "He knew everything that was going on at that campus," Paknis argued. "For him to state he didn't know, or that he was not aware, it's total denial. That whole community was in denial. If this would have come out in 1998, Joe would've been out, or his name would have been tarnished. They tried to push it under the rug as long as possible. Joe is the dean, the master. How could he not have known? A fish rots from the head first. The image was more important than the health and well-being of kids."

Barry Switzer, a former coach of the University of Oklahoma Sooners as well as the NFL's Dallas Cowboys, told the *Oklahoman,* the largest daily newspaper in the state, that he believed Paterno must have known. "Having been in this profession a long time and knowing how close coaching staffs are, I knew that this was a secret that was kept secret. Everyone on that staff had to have known."

Perhaps more damning, a Pennsylvania state trooper with knowledge of the Sandusky investigation insisted that Paterno had to have been savvy to at least the big picture, if not the details. "It's a no-brainer. He knew what the light bill was in that place," the trooper said.

Then came 2002, when Assistant Coach Mike McQueary contacted Paterno after he witnessed what he called a sexual act between Sandusky and a ten-year-old boy. Paterno waited a day before he contacted Athletic Director Tim Curley. "I contacted my superiors and I said, 'Hey we got a problem, I think. Would you guys look into it?' " Paterno told the *Washington Post* in his last published interview. Asked why he didn't follow up more aggressively, he said, "I didn't know exactly how to handle it and I was afraid to do something that might jeopardize what the university procedure was. So I backed away and turned it over to some other people, people I thought would have a little more expertise than I did. It didn't work out that way."

CHAPTER TWELVE

SANDUSKY SPEAKS

NBC's Bob Costas knew it was a big deal—the proverbial exclusive—when Joseph Amendola, the lawyer for the accused pedophile Jerry Sandusky, agreed to appear on a segment of NBC's prime-time news magazine program *Rock Center with Brian Williams*. In later interviews Costas said he had little time before Amendola was due to arrive, about three hours before the show, so he quickly read and reread a wide assortment of reporting surrounding charges against Sandusky. He knew Amendola was there to dispute the indictment's contention that Sandusky was a serial child predator whose deeds were covered up by Penn State officials for more than a decade. He could not foresee how the exclusive he already owned would reveal more than anyone anticipated.

The standard was that before a trial criminal defense lawyers usually didn't render much more than a few carefully crafted sound bites declaring the innocence of their client. But Amendola had been different. From the start of the case, Sandusky's lawyer had directed a public frontal assault against the damning charges and the accusers who brought them.

As the two men sat in the studio waiting for the cameras to roll, Costas learned that Amendola was conducting his own investigation into the charges filed against Sandusky in early November 2011. Before they went on the air, he told Costas they had already tracked down some supposed victims of Sandusky's assaults. Contrary to what prosecutors contended in a twenty-three-page presentment filled with allegations of insidious abuse at Sandusky's hands, Amendola said some of the young men were going to testify that he had never done a thing to them. Then, just before the taped interview was to begin, Amendola blew Costas away with a proposal: Would he like to interview Jerry Sandusky himself? Costas quickly accepted. Within minutes he had Sandusky on the phone for his first interview, an exclusive about the sex abuse scandal enveloping him and Penn State.

The interview happened so quickly and so close to the 8 P.M. airtime that the network hardly had time to promote it. Nevertheless the November 14, 2011, interview would create great consternation and controversy. The show's ratings spiked, and the interview quickly went viral on the Internet.

COSTAS OPENED THE INTERVIEW BLUNTLY. "Mr. Sandusky, there's a forty-count indictment. The Grand Jury report contains specific detail. There are multiple accusers, multiple eyewitnesses to various aspects of the abuse. A reasonable person says where there's this much smoke, there must be plenty of fire. What do you say?"

Sandusky's response was equally to the point: "I say that I am innocent of those charges."

"Innocent? Completely innocent and falsely accused in every aspect?" Costas asked.

"Well, I could say that, you know, I have done some of those things. I have horsed around with kids. I have showered after workouts. I have hugged them and I have touched their leg, without intent of sexual contact. But—so if you look at it that way—there are things that wouldn't, you know, would be accurate."

"Are you denying that you had any inappropriate sexual contact with any of these underage boys?"

"I, yes, yes, I am," Sandusky answered hesitantly.

"Never touched their genitals? Never engaged in oral sex?"

"Right."

Costas tried to bring other known significant witnesses into his line of questioning. "What about Mike McQueary, the grad assistant who in 2002 walked into the shower where he says in specific detail that you were forcibly raping a boy who appeared to be ten or eleven years old? That his hands were up against the shower wall and he heard rhythmic slap, slap, slapping sounds and he described that as a rape?"

"I would say that that's false," said Sandusky with questionable conviction.

"What would be his motive to lie?" Costas wanted to know.

"You'd have to ask him that."

"What did happen in the shower the night that Mike McQueary happened upon you and the young boy?"

Sandusky stammered through the answer to that question. "Okay, we—we were showering and—and horsing around. And he actually turned all the showers on and was—actually sliding—across the—the floor. And we were—as I recall possibly like snapping a towel, horseplay."

Costas wanted to know if in 1998 a mother had confronted him about taking a shower with her son and inappropriately touching him. He wanted to know also about the two detectives who had eavesdropped on the conversation. "What happened there?" he asked.

"I can't exactly recall what was said there. In terms of—what I did say was that if he felt that way, then I was wrong."

"During one of those conversations, you said, 'I understand, I was wrong, I wish I could get forgiveness,' speaking now with the mother. 'I know I won't get it from you. I wish I were dead.' A guy falsely accused or a guy whose actions have been misinterpreted doesn't respond that way, does he?"

"I don't know. I didn't say, to my recollection, that I wish I were dead. I was hopeful that we could reconcile things."

Costas brought up the eyewitness report of a janitor. "Shortly after that, in 2000, a janitor said that he saw you performing oral sex on a young boy in the showers, in the Penn State locker facility. Did that happen?"

Sandusky said no.

Costas wanted to know why somebody would think he saw something so extreme and shocking if it hadn't occurred. As with his response to Costas's question about McQueary, Sandusky said he'd have to ask the janitor.

Costas pushed on. "It seems that if all of these accusations are false, you are the unluckiest and most persecuted man that any of us has ever heard about."

Sandusky laughed. "I don't know what you want me to say." He agreed that these hadn't been the best days of his life.

As Sandusky remained on the line, Costas turned to Amendola. "You said a few days ago 'Much more is going to come out in our defense.' In broad terms, what?"

"We expect we're going to have a number of kids. Now how many of those so-called eight kids, we're not sure. But we anticipate we're going to have at least several of those kids come forward and say this never happened. . . . In fact, one of the toughest allegations—the McQueary violations, what McQueary said he saw—we have information that that child says that never happened. Now grown up . . . now the person's in his twenties."

"Until now, we were told that that alleged victim could not be identified. . . . So you found him, the commonwealth has not?"

"Interesting, isn't it?" Amendola responded.

Costas challenged Amendola, asking him if he would allow his own children to be alone with Sandusky. Amendola answered without hesitation. "Absolutely," he declared. "I believe in Jerry's innocence. Quite honestly, Bob, that's why I'm involved in the case."

Costas ended the interview with a few more questions to Sandusky about Joe Paterno. He wanted to know if Paterno had ever spoken to him directly about the allegations regarding his behavior. Sandusky said no, he never had. Costas wanted to know about the fallout of Sandusky's behavior on Penn State, the football program, and Joe Paterno personally. Sandusky answered, "How would you think that I would feel about a university that I attended, about people that I've worked with, about people that I care so much about? . . . I feel horrible."

"You feel horrible. Do you feel culpable?"

"I'm not sure I know what you mean."

"Do you feel guilty? Do you feel as if it's your fault?"

"Guilty?" Sandusky parroted, puzzled. "No, I don't think it's my fault. I've obviously played a part in this."

". . . What are you willing to concede that you've done that was wrong and you wish you had not done it?" Costas asked.

Again, Sandusky was hesitant. "Well, in retrospect, I—you know, I shouldn't have showered with those kids. You know."

"That's it?" Costas asked.

"Well, that—yeah, that's what hits me the most."

"Are you a pedophile?"

"No," Sandusky replied.

"Are you sexually attracted to young boys, to underage boys?"

Sandusky had trouble with that one. He needed clarification. "Am I sexually attracted to underage boys?"

"Yes," Costas said.

"Sexually attracted, you know, I enjoy young people. I love to be around them. But no, I'm not sexually attracted to young boys."

Costas continued giving him the benefit of the doubt. "Obviously you're entitled to a presumption of innocence and you'll receive a vigorous defense. On the other hand, there is a tremendous amount of information out there and fair-minded commonsense people have concluded that you are guilty of monstrous acts. And they are particularly unforgiving with the type of crimes that have been alleged here. And so millions of Americans who didn't know Jerry Sandusky's name until a week ago now regard you not only as a criminal, but, I say this, I think, in a considered way, but as some sort of monster. How do you respond to them?"

"I don't know what I can say that would make anybody feel any different now. I would just say that if somehow people could hang out until my attorney has a chance to fight, you know, for my innocence. That's about all I could ask right now. And you know, obviously, it's a huge challenge."

Costas thanked him for his time and the interview ended. Immediately the Internet was filled with commentary about why Sandusky would agree to take questions and why Amendola would allow it. In terms of specifics, bloggers were most curious about what took the disgraced coach so long to answer the question about sexually desiring young boys. They were shocked that he explained himself rather than just saying no. Newspaper reports were loaded with defense lawyers and child abuse experts who characterized that nonspecific answer as evidence affirming Sandusky's prurient interests. His denials also sparked outrage from his accusers and their lawyers. The outrage alternated between castigation of Amendola for allowing the interview and anger over Sandusky's across-the-board denials.

"This is one of the worst cases of voyeurism I've ever seen," said Marci Hamilton, a lawyer and expert in child abuse cases who, at the time, was preparing a lawsuit she would later file on behalf of a man who said Sandusky assaulted him one hundred times. She could not understand why Amendola would put his client on national television before he was tried. Ultimately, she said, it was Sandusky's choice, even if in her opinion it was a bad one for legal reasons. "The beauty of this was that once he began talking about taking showers with children, anyone who listened would see he doesn't get it, that he's so deeply involved in the world of child abuse and his own narcissism that he has an inability to understand how his message plays out with healthy adults. It is very typical [of child predators]," Hamilton said.

Andrew Shubin, a Pennsylvania lawyer who represented at least one of the young men, issued a written statement after the interview aired: "Our investigation reveals that Sandusky is an unrepentant child predator. He caused incalculable devastation to children, their families and our community and is continuing to do so through his attacks on the victims' credibility."

Justine Andronici, a victim's rights lawyer who is working with Shubin and others on the Sandusky case, also lashed out in a statement of her own: "These statements play on the victims' worst fears—that if they stand up and tell the truth they will be called liars and victimized again. Pedophiles seek to silence their victims with the threat that no one will believe them if they come forward. Perpetrators of sexual abuse also maintain manipulative, long-term contact with their victims for the very purpose of continuing to silence them."

Michael Boni, the lawyer representing the Clinton County boy whose reports to state police started the grand jury investigation in 2008, said Sandusky's interview with Costas felt like "another punch in the stomach" to his client and his client's mother.

As if letting Costas have access to Sandusky weren't enough, Amendola made his client available to the *New York Times* two weeks later. With his lawyer in the room, Sandusky talked for four hours over two days. He repeated many of the things he had told Costas, but he also tried to explain why he did not quickly and directly answer the question about whether he is attracted to young boys. "I'm sitting there saying, 'What in the world is this question?' If I say, 'No, I'm not attracted to boys,' that's not the truth, because I'm attracted to young people—boys, girls."

Sandusky's lawyer could be heard in the background chiming in to help him with the answer. "Yeah, but not sexually," Amendola said. "You're attracted because you enjoy spending time [with them]."

Sandusky picked up the hint. "Right," he agreed. "That's what I was trying to say. I enjoy spending time with young people."

Later Amendola said he was considering scheduling another network interview so Sandusky and his wife, Dottie, could defend against numerous allegations that children had been abused in their home, sometimes while Dottie was upstairs. The couple wanted to say the allegations were patently untrue.

The indictment did not directly implicate Dottie Sandusky, but she was mentioned in it. The presentment said she was in contact with at least two former Second Milers during the grand jury investigation. Like most of the others, the young man listed in the presentment as Victim 7 said he was abused repeatedly in Sandusky's basement bedroom. According to the indictment, in the summer of 2011 he "had not had contact with Sandusky for nearly two years but was contacted by Sandusky, and separately by his wife and a friend in the weeks prior to Victim 7's appearance before the Grand Jury. The callers left messages saying the matter was very important. Victim 7 did not return these phone calls."

Also during the summer of 2011, after Sandusky had resigned from the charity under the cloud of the grand jury investigation, he and his wife invited the child later known as Victim 6 to dinner under the guise of hosting a get-together for Second Mile alumni. Victim 6 was the child whose mother reported Sandusky to police in 1998 after her son told her he'd inappropriately shared a shower with Sandusky in the Penn State football locker room. The boy's lawyer and the Pennsylvania State Police discussed the Sandusky proposition with the child. If he was up to the task, they would send him with a wire and keep the residence under surveillance to protect him. The young man agreed to the sting, but said he was too afraid to wear a wire. He met for dinner with Jerry and Dottie; however, they did not discuss the grand jury.

After the interview with the *New York Times*, Amendola continued to say that the allegations were false. There was always so much activity in the Sandusky home when the children visited that the abuse described in the charges could never have happened, he said.

Dottie Sandusky had been a mother figure to The Second Mile for decades. While Jerry was still coaching, she was left to do the heavy lifting at home. The in-season demands on her husband's time and his constant traveling throughout the year for football-related events and recruitment of players made her a football widow. Jerry joked that he was another kid for her to supervise; that's why he affectionately called her "Sarge," according to his autobiography.

While she did make contact with grand jury witnesses in the summer of 2011, it remains unclear if she knew about the full range of the accusations against her husband, including the abuse reports from 1998 and 2002. A friend of some of the Sandusky children thought she knew more than she was letting on. He told a newspaper reporter for the *Centre Daily Times* that Dottie had once discussed with him her long-standing concern that her husband's touchy-feely behavior toward children might one day cause someone to take him the wrong way.

She took her first and only public stand in a written statement after a second set of charges was filed against her husband on December 7, 2011, in relation to two more accusers who came forward with allegations of sexual abuse against Sandusky. One of the accusers suggested Dottie may have known her husband was molesting him in their basement. According to the presentment, that young man said he was told to stay in the basement during his visits to the Sandusky home. He said Sandusky delivered his meals to him there and that he was repeatedly abused and raped by Sandusky in the finished basement bedroom. Most disturbingly, he said while he was being anally raped "on at least one occasion he screamed for help, knowing that Sandusky's wife was upstairs, but no one ever came to help him."

That allegation that Dottie may have ignored a sexual assault in her basement provoked Dottie's only public statement. In a letter to the press, Dottie vehemently defended her husband and addressed the young man's allegations: "I have been shocked and dismayed by the allegations made against Jerry, particularly the most recent one that a young man has said he was kept in our basement during visits and screamed for help as Jerry assaulted him while I was in our home and didn't respond to his cries for help. As the mother of six children, I have been devastated by these accusations. I am also angry about these false accusations that such a terrible incident ever occurred in my home."

Dottie insisted that all the hundreds of children who visited their home over the years were treated like family. She said her own family and friends could vouch for their good care of children. She finished by thanking all of their supporters and saying Jerry would prove his innocence.

Dottie hasn't been seen in public much since, although she had to wade through a sea of cameras on December 7, when she came to district court after a second set of charges was filed against her husband. Two more young men had come forward with allegations of abuse, and a judge remanded him to jail, pending a $250,000 cash bond. Dottie had to sign over the deed to their house and put up as collateral a $50,000 cashier's check to secure her husband's release. She and her husband were also seen, surrounded by several members of their family, when they arrived at the Centre County Courthouse in early December 2011 for Sandusky's preliminary hearing. Dottie's full head of red hair had faded to gray, and the vibrant smile present when cameras caught her in good times had turned into a stoic frown. She followed her husband into court peering straight ahead. She did not utter a word, as if there were nothing more she could say.

CHAPTER THIRTEEN

THE COURT OF
PUBLIC OPINION

Before dawn on December 12, 2011, more than two hundred reporters crowded into the Centre County Courthouse in bucolic Bellefonte, Pennsylvania, almost two hours before Jerry Sandusky was expected to face as many as ten young accusers prepared to testify under oath that he was a predatory pedophile. Outside the steepled courthouse at least twice that many photographers and television technicians were jammed onto a frozen patch of lawn that had been painted with red lines to give every network a piece of earth from which to broadcast their reports about one of the most infamous child sex abuse cases in American history. A representative from Oprah Winfrey was passing out handwritten letters to lawyers from the television impresario asking for exclusive interviews with their clients. More than thirteen hundred people had registered for a lottery for one of a hundred courtroom seats available to the general public. The overflow crowd could watch the proceedings via closed circuit television in a county office building across the street. In an unprecedented ruling, a visiting judge allowed reporters to bring laptop computers into the courtroom to transmit minute-by-minute accounts of the proceedings via Twitter and other social networks.

Never before had security in Bellefonte, a town of just over six thousand people, been so tight. The Centre County seat, which got its name from a natural spring buried deep below it, was better known for fly-fishing than courtroom drama. But on this crisp morning heavily armed local and state police surrounded the courthouse. Snipers with high-powered rifles scanned the scene from perches behind Victorian eaves on the roofs of historic buildings, whose unique charm was normally fodder for walking tours led by architecture enthusiasts.

About an hour before the hearing was to begin on that subfreezing morning, Jerry Sandusky emerged from a vehicle in a back lot and smiled briefly as his grim-faced wife gripped his arm and walked silently beside him. A tan shawl shielded her from the cold, and white pearls adorned her ears. The gray-haired grandmother with wire-rimmed glasses added nothing to written statements she had given in the weeks leading up to the hearing, when she had offered full support for her husband of forty years.

As the couple walked deliberately toward the front steps of the courthouse, neither they nor those who had come out to support them this cold winter day avoided the cameras, but they all ignored questions. Sandusky's smile had vanished by the time he went through the metal detector and made the solemn walk to the upstairs courtroom. The room was quiet as Dottie and other family members veered to the right to find their reserved seats. Sandusky walked behind his lawyer, Joseph Amendola, who glad-handed attorneys and reporters as he waltzed up the courtroom aisle like a politician on the campaign trail. Sandusky made no eye contact with anyone, instead gazing blankly ahead or occasionally up at the painted gold leaves crowning the ceiling.

Two young men sat silently in a courthouse anteroom just a few feet from where they expected to take the witness stand and unburden themselves of terrible secrets. Eight other young men sat in a private conference room in a state police barracks outside of town, ready to report to the courthouse accompanied by undercover state troopers when it was their turn to testify. All of them were being consoled by their lawyers, who had prepped them extensively during the past week for what they could expect. Some had known each other from picnics and swimming meets and other programs they experienced as young children at The Second Mile; others had met as they awaited their turn on a psychologist's couch. A few of them were there because their mothers had called police when they learned of Sandusky's misdeeds; most of them had never intended to face down the man. They had merely answered questions when investigators asked if they had experienced inappropriate behavior by Sandusky.

The young men were not from the same towns in central Pennsylvania, but they were bonded by common threads in their backgrounds. All of them had troubled family situations or had been in trouble at school. All of them went to The Second Mile because it offered programs and people who would help them build needed structure in their lives. They also learned through the program to develop a positive outlook to face their adversities.

To the outside world, they would be identified by the collective label of "victim" in the Sandusky case and assigned numbers one through ten to tell them apart. But inside the conference room they had faces and names and personalities that made them flesh-and-blood human beings. They also had another thing in common: all of them had told a statewide investigating grand jury they had been sexually assaulted by Sandusky after they turned to or were sent by school counselors to The Second Mile. They had sworn under oath that once Sandusky identified them as marks for abuse, he plied them with material things they previously could only dream of. In each case, the boys thought they had found a male role model who genuinely cared about them. Now they were prepared to say in open court that Sandusky had made inappropriate sexual advances toward them and in some cases that he had molested them for months or years.

That morning they all felt the underlying tension. They would have to stare down the jovial, white-haired Sandusky and tell a judge that the man who professed to love them had betrayed their trust and stolen their souls. All of them had been advised not to share the details of their sexual molestation at the hands of Sandusky. They didn't need to. By that point all of them had read the original forty-count indictment as well as the twelve additional counts against their former mentor. All of them now understood that Sandusky was being accused with crafting a grooming plan of abuse as tightly as he had strategies for defensive success on the gridiron. They now knew they weren't alone in their nightmares.

The plan put together by prosecutors called for the first two witnesses already in the courthouse to complete their testimony. Then the rest would be driven one by one from the state police barracks to face down Sandusky. Some of these young men had waited fifteen years to break their silence. They waited because they feared Sandusky, or were so ashamed of what he had done to them that they preferred to keep it secret, or were convinced no one would believe them. Now the day had finally come to confront their internal and external demons in front of a national audience.

In the days leading up to this first showdown, Amendola worked the media in an effort to knock down the seriousness of charges against his client. He proclaimed to almost any reporter who asked that Sandusky was innocent and that his actions had been misunderstood. Sandusky himself had given two interviews, in which he admitted that he had showered with boys and had engaged in contact that others would, at the very least, deem inappropriate. Sandusky's actions, Amendola argued, were not sexual but the acts of an "overgrown kid." Amendola, who pointedly referred to the young men as "accusers," stated that as many as half of them might be called to testify as character witnesses on Sandusky's behalf.

The courtroom audience couldn't wait to hear the evidence and listen to the voices of young men whose stories had only been told in printed statements from the Pennsylvania attorney general's office. Before Sandusky even took his seat, Amendola led him into a back room for a meeting with prosecutors. Fifteen minutes later the two men emerged. The man who had been pictured in news reports for years pumping his fists and smiling broadly after college football victories slumped forlornly into his seat at the defense table. His head drooped as if he couldn't summon the strength to hold it up, his hands folded on the table in front of him.

After a quick and hushed meeting in front of Senior Magisterial District Judge Robert E. Scott, Sandusky's lawyer announced that his client would waive his preliminary hearing and take his case directly to trial. In less than two minutes after Sandusky told the judge he agreed with the waiver the hearing was over.

People inside and outside the courtroom were stunned. If his intention had been to waive the hearing, why had he waited until the last minute and put all his alleged victims through the horrible process of preparing to testify? One possible scenario was that Sandusky, the ultimate control freak, wanted to let the process go forward only to be the ultimate director of the action. Caught by reporters as he exited a back door of the courthouse, Sandusky was resolute and offered a football metaphor as a sound bite: "We fully intend to put together the best possible defense that we can do, to stay the course, to fight for four quarters. . . . We want the opportunity to present our side."

Reporters had expected a full day or more in court and testimony from as many as ten of Sandusky's accusers. Now they had to chase after Amendola, who was ready and more than willing to present his case in the court of public opinion in front of a forest of microphones on the front lawn of the courthouse.

Amendola said he had legitimate reasons for waiting until trial to contest the charges. First of all, he said, rules of preliminary hearings in Pennsylvania courts limit cross-examination of witnesses. Prosecutors have to present only enough evidence that a crime had occurred, known as *prima facie*, or first blush, to cause the matter to be held for trial. In talks late the previous night, he said, prosecutors agreed to quickly turn over discovery materials, a legal term that describes the state's obligation to turn over all evidence in the cases against Sandusky, especially any negative information they possess about any potential witnesses. He said they also agreed that if future charges were to be filed against his client, prosecutors would not ask for a higher bond.

In reality, however, Amendola had another reason for waiving the case to trial. He knew testimony from a parade of accusers would become fodder for a second media onslaught against his client that wouldn't end for weeks. Although the media storm technically had nothing to do with what happened inside the courtroom, Amendola wanted to curb the tide of negative publicity, so he continued performing his own monumental spin job. There were no plea bargains under way, and he was eager to take the case to trial, he chirped into a public address system in front of the courthouse. In a point-by-point rebuttal of charges and wide-ranging accusations against Sandusky's accusers, Amendola answered questions for over an hour. He admitted that while his client was prepared to fight, he was "depressed": "He's devastated because everything he has done in his life, all of the good things, have been turned upside down." Meanwhile Sandusky was driven back home.

As for the young men who had accused him of pedophilia, Amendola said both Sandusky and his wife were mystified. They had always considered some of those boys part of their extended family. He also said the Sanduskys had spent time in the past year with at least two of the accusers, not knowing the young men were preparing to testify before the grand jury or had already done so. He scoffed at the presentment's implication that those contacts were veiled efforts to intimidate the young men.

Amendola agreed with a questioner who said that the burdens on the defense were akin to climbers starting a hike to reach the summit of Mount Everest. He took no mercy on anyone who had any accusatory things to say about his client. He argued that some of the accusations against Sandusky didn't remotely involve sexual contact. Showering with a boy after a workout might seem odd, Amendola said, but it did not rise to the level of a crime. He failed to address the perverse things his client was alleged to have done with the young boys in the shower.

Amendola reserved his most damning commentary for Mike Mc-Queary. It was McQueary who testified to the grand jury that he saw Sandusky molesting a ten-year-old boy. Despite the fact that there were at least ten accusers against Sandusky, Amendola characterized McQueary as the "centerpiece" of the state's case against his client. He said he believed McQueary's testimony was the reason charges were pursued against Sandusky, Tim Curley, and Gary Schultz. Amendola also said it was McQueary's statements that led to the ouster of Joe Paterno and Graham Spanier.

Amendola claimed that although the grand jury considered McQueary's testimony "extremely credible," information since then had shown major inconsistencies in what the assistant coach, now on paid leave, saw and did. He said that questions about whether McQueary stopped the alleged assault, whether he reported it to police, exactly what he told Paterno, Curley, and Schultz, and a variety of other issues had been raised since the release of the grand jury's presentment. He had found so many inconsistencies that he could "wipe [McQueary] off of this case." Sandusky's attorney found it unbelievable and unimaginable that McQueary went into a locker room, witnessed Sandusky anally assaulting a ten-year-old boy, but did nothing to come to the child's aid and didn't call police. The fact that he instead went home to tell his father, who then suggested he take the matter to Paterno instead of the police, was also highly questionable. He said another of McQueary's stories also didn't make sense: in one version he told Curley and Schultz specific sexual details of the shower encounter, and in another, milder version he mentioned only "horsing around" and "horseplay." Amendola insisted that Curley and Schultz, who he called decent and conservative men, would not have reacted to serious criminal behaviors such as child rape with a mild admonishment to Sandusky to stop taking showers with children. "If you believe that, I suggest you dial 1-800-REALITY," Amendola said, not realizing that number is for a pay-per-call phone service offering gay and bisexual pornography.

Amendola charged that the accusers were driven by the chance to make money off Sandusky. He pointed to the ranks of personal injury and civil rights lawyers present that day to support his claim. He suspected collusion among the accusers, all bent on a big payday from lawsuits against Penn State and The Second Mile. One of the first things he was going to do was investigate whether the young men who made the allegations against Sandusky knew each other. He planned to seek records of text messages, telephone calls, and other data to see if they had had contact with each other. "We're ready to defend, always have been ready to defend," he said.

Amendola's comments brought quick and specific rebukes, also on the courthouse lawn, from the pack of lawyers he chastised. Just as he had done, the lawyers of the young men made the rounds from CNN to NBC, CBS, ABC, and virtually every print and Internet news organization in

America to challenge the assertions of Sandusky's lawyer and to buttress the resolve of their clients.

Among them was Ben Andreozzi, one of the lawyers for the young man identified as Victim 4, who was to be the first witness to face Sandusky at his preliminary hearing. Andreozzi said his client, who had suffered long-term abuse from Sandusky, had experienced a range of emotions. Initially he had had no desire to become involved in the trial. Then he became terrified about testifying but had found the inner resolve to step up. After he learned the preliminary hearing was waived, the young man gave Andreozzi a handwritten statement to be read to the media: "This is the most difficult time of my life. I can't put into words how unbearable this has been on my life, both physically and mentally. I can't believe they put us through this until the last second only to waive the hearing. I want to thank all of the people who have shown support. Regardless of the decision to waive the hearing, nothing has changed. I will still stand my ground, testify and speak the truth." Andreozzi pointed out that the young man underlined the word "truth" three times in his statement. "I do think it is important to see what the victims are going through," Andreozzi said.

Lawyers for other victims offered some insights about depression, drug and alcohol abuse, and other mental health issues their clients had battled. Some of the young men had found it difficult to focus on careers because Sandusky had destroyed their psyches, the attorneys said. On the other hand, lawyers for at least two of the accusers said their clients had earned college degrees and built careers and relationships despite their scars. It had taken years of introspection to move ahead, but most had persevered, not knowing there were others who faced the same issues.

As for collusion, Andreozzi said his client had apologized to some of the younger accusers for not having the courage to come forward sooner. If Amendola wanted to score him over that, "then shame on him." "To suggest these young men should not be in communication with each other is somewhat disingenuous. I think it is important for their recovery to have the opportunity at some point to share their stories in a group session."

On the issue of a financial windfall, Andreozzi said he had represented his client for nearly a year prior to the indictments. He figured Sandusky had few unencumbered assets, so the odds were slim of ever reaping a significant financial settlement. He said he did not learn that prosecutors had also accused Penn State and The Second Mile of a cover-up—which could make them liable for damages in civil court—until he read the grand jury presentment.

Two of the lawyers representing Victim 6 called Sandusky "a coward" for waiving the hearing. Their client was the child whose mother had first reported Sandusky in 1998 for showering naked with her son in the Penn State football locker room. "Anyone who would abuse a child is by definition a coward," said one of the attorneys, Ken Suggs, as reporters crowded around him. Suggs and his co-counsel, Howard Janet, said that after their client's mother reported Sandusky to police, Sandusky admitted what he had done and ultimately said his life as he knew it was over. "The guy said he wished he was dead," said Janet.

Janet acknowledged that his client had dined with Sandusky and his wife in the summer of 2011, but as to being called as a character witness for Sandusky, he said nothing could be further from the truth. "It is grotesque that Sandusky or his lawyer would suggest that a victim of molestation attending a dinner Sandusky invited him to is somehow a defense to the indefensible actions of which Sandusky has been accused." Victim 6 had not seen Sandusky for many years when he got a call from the man, who had known for more than two years that he was the subject of a grand jury probe. That was in July 2011, just four months before Sandusky would be indicted. Almost all of the evidence had been presented. Sandusky, according to the young man's lawyer, invited his client to dinner. Sandusky pitched the dinner "to prospective attendees as an opportunity to catch up with former Second Mile participants," even though he had resigned from the charity two years earlier.

Janet said authorities investigating Sandusky were notified and had given their seal of approval for Victim 6 to attend. "They even wanted him to wear an electronic listening device. Though he opted not to wear the 'wire' because he was nervous about doing so, he reported details back to law enforcement."

According to Janet and Suggs, more questions than answers emerged

from Sandusky's dinner with their client. They would later post them on
the firm's website: "Why was he arranging to meet with victims while under
investigation? Was he trying to tamper with or improperly influence potential witnesses? Was he trying to use the victims' attendance at dinner to
discredit their accusations against him as part of a devious strategic plan of
defense? Did he plan all along to try to influence the public or the jury pool
by pointing to victim's attendance at the dinner? Why did he keep showering these children with gifts and access to Penn State football games long
after they left The Second Mile and had become adults? Does he truly
believe that 'relationships' can be built on the sort of inappropriate interactions he is accused of initiating with these boys?"

   The lawyers, who represent child victims nationally, said their client
was intent on telling the truth when he took the witness stand. "Hopefully,
as a result of Victim 6 and others having the courage to come forward,
not only will justice be done, but it will aid in their healing. We have a responsibility to shine a bright light on the practice of 'grooming' vulnerable
children for sexual activity—especially when it is enabled by institutional
indifference. Today we call on Sandusky and his lawyer to stop the manipu-
lation and mental abuse of these former Second Mile children and Penn
State devotees so that this matter may be resolved quickly and healing may
get underway."

   As for the client he represents, Janet has said the twenty-seven-year-
old had not decided if he wanted to file a civil suit in the matter. The
young man, who has become deeply religious since his experiences with
Sandusky, had no plans to do anything about the abuse he suffered until
investigators visited him. That's when he contacted Janet. At the time he
did not know there were other victims of Sandusky's abuse. Janet said one
of the most profound moments of the entire chain of events came when
Victim 6 finally got a chance to read the twenty-three-page presentment
against Sandusky. His lawyer said he was devastated. "He cried. He didn't
cry for what happened to him. He cried for the others."

   Tom Kline of the Philadelphia law firm Kline and Specter would not
reveal which of the alleged victims he represented. Kline said the day was a
seminal event for Sandusky's accusers. It enabled them to come away from

the hearing with a feeling of mutual support, even though technically nothing had happened. "That whole day was one where they all realized there
was strength in numbers. Anybody who had any reservations about coming
forward who went through that process became steadfast in their determination to see it through." Kline suggested the coalescing of energy among
those readying themselves to testify was bad for Sandusky in the short and
long run. That was especially true for most of the accusers, who did not
seek the public light or revenge against Sandusky, but got involved after "a
knock at the door" from investigators in late 2010 or early 2011. Now all of
them knew they were not alone.

Amendola didn't hear the rebukes from the alleged victims' lawyers
because he was still doing interviews across the courthouse lawn. Later he
said he talked as much as he could because his client had been crucified
around the world. He wanted to achieve some balance in coverage so folks
would have an open mind about his client. He said he planned to try the
case in Centre County because extensive pretrial publicity was so pervasive
around the nation there really was no other place to take it. He admitted
the stakes were high: "This is the fight of Jerry Sandusky's life and we plan
to fight this to the death."

CHAPTER FOURTEEN

——

THE GREAT PRETENDER

Jerry Sandusky certainly had the credentials to become the head football coach at other universities. He owned two national championship rings for coaching the defenses of the 1982 and 1986 Penn State teams that had finished No. 1 in the country, and as the reigning Dean of Linebacker U., he was feeding the National Football League a steady flow of linebackers and other defensive talent. Potential employers noticed and called with head coach job opportunities. In the years following Penn State's second championship, Sandusky was wooed by Boston College, Temple University, the University of Maryland, and the University of Virginia. Whether or not he turned them all down or didn't get the job after all, Sandusky remained at Penn State as a subordinate to Joe Paterno. The reason for staying, Sandusky would say, was that he loved the small-town atmosphere of State College surrounding the big-time football success at Penn State, and he loved the nurturing relationships with the at-risk kids being referred to his charity. But was there an ulterior motive in spurning outside offers? Did The Second Mile provide him, as the supporting documents of his indictment charged, with a renewable and overlapping supply of prey in a pedophile pipeline? Did he use the Penn State campus he professed to love as a personal playground to groom youngsters for sinister purposes?

Lawyers and counselors of sexual abuse victims have said that Sandusky's inappropriate relationships with boys dated back to shortly after he founded The Second Mile as a group home in 1977. The indictments and lawsuits contain accounts that start in 1992. Each young man thought he had a special relationship with Sandusky. Each thought he was the only one targeted as Sandusky built a bond of trust over time and then double-crossed him. Each of the boys' relationships with Sandusky ended when they grew up, moved on, or found excuses to end their bond with him.

One young man who has filed a lawsuit in Philadelphia against Sandusky but was not among those who testified before the investigating grand jury, said he had been referred to The Second Mile in 1992, when he was ten years old. He said Sandusky took him to Penn State football facilities and Nittany Lions' games, and he was also Sandusky's guest at football games played by the Philadelphia Eagles. In his lawsuit, the young man said he was sexually abused more than one hundred times by Sandusky at Penn State facilities or at Sandusky's home in State College. The abuse continued for four years, through 1996. He kept the abuse secret for more than fifteen years because Sandusky threatened to harm his family if he ever told anyone, according to the lawsuit.

Another young man said under oath to the statewide investigating grand jury that in 1994, when he was ten years old, a school counselor had recommended that he attend the programs offered by The Second Mile. He was warmly welcomed to the program by the jovial mentor and founder. The young man said that when he rode in Sandusky's Cadillac, the coach would touch him improperly, rubbing his leg and putting his hand down his pants en route to sporting events and workouts. Inappropriate contact was also made in the football locker room in Holuba Hall on the Penn State campus and in the basement bedroom of Sandusky's house, where the former coach would lie down behind the boy and envelope him in his arms.

If this child's abuse began in 1994, as he has alleged, Sandusky would already have been abusing the boy who filed suit in Philadelphia who claimed his assaults lasted from 1992 through 1996. This is a common modus operandi for serial pedophiles. When one boy is aging toward adolescence, the pedophile will groom a younger one to replace him when the time is right.

During the same time period that Sandusky was allegedly abusing and grooming these two young men between 1995 and 1996, he showed special interest in an eight-year-old boy in The Second Mile program. Sandusky made him his guest at more than a dozen football games before he began making sexual overtures. The young man said he was taken to the football facilities at Holuba Hall when no one else was present. He described how Sandusky had playfully pushed him around in a sauna and then taken him to a shower, where the coach touched him with his erect penis, the boy said. He said he escaped the coach's grasp and then asked to be taken home. Sandusky never invited him to another event.

The young man who was scheduled to be the first witness to testify at Sandusky's preliminary hearing said he was shown much affection when he had first met the coach through The Second Mile, when he was twelve or thirteen in 1996 or 1997. His relationship with Sandusky was not abnormal for three years, and Sandusky even invited him to a family picnic. But one day Sandusky grabbed him inappropriately when the two of them were playing around in a swimming pool. Sexual abuse later occurred in the Penn State football showers and eventually at Sandusky's home, the young man said.

Even the Sandusky football routine seemed to fit Sandusky's purposes. On nights before home games, the Nittany Lions stayed at the Toftrees Resort and Conference Center right in State College. Toftrees was a perfect hideaway. It was located within ten minutes of Beaver Stadium, yet it was isolated on a 1500-acre parcel of land away from the Friday night Penn State rah-rah. Curfew was a lot easier to enforce at Toftrees than it would have been in campus dormitories. Sandusky invited the young man to stay with him at Toftrees and sexually abused him there, according to prosecutors. In addition, Sandusky had the young man join his family on bowl games to Orlando, Florida, in 1998 and San Antonio, Texas, in 1999.

He said Sandusky visited his room in the team hotel on the Texas trip and threated to send him home if sexual advances were refused, according to the documents supporting the criminal charges made against Sandusky.

The number of children alleging abuse in the same time period is revoltingly mind-blowing. Also in 1997, yet another boy said he was lured into Sandusky's secret world. The boy was eleven and had been experiencing personal problems at home. A school counselor had referred him to The Second Mile. Sandusky knew of the child's issues at home and took an immediate interest in him. Within a short time Sandusky's behavior became intimate. He said he was hugged, rubbed, cuddled, and tickled. When he was invited to sleep over at Sandusky's house, the boy was overjoyed. But he was soon horrified when he was molested in the basement bedroom by the man who acted like a father to him, the young man said. The abuse lasted for three years, according to the boy. He said he endured being repeatedly forced to perform oral sex on Sandusky and was raped at least sixteen times. Most disturbing was this contention, according to the grand jury presentment: "On at least one occasion he screamed for help, knowing that Sandusky's wife was upstairs, but no one came to help him."

It is unclear if the alleged abuse of this boy was still going on in May 1998, when another child came home with wet hair after an evening with Sandusky. It was this child's mother who called Penn State campus police to set the 1998 investigation in motion. It is saddening now to recall Sandusky's promise to the boy's mother after that investigation was fizzling that he would never shower with her son or any other child again. That a grown man got a pass after showering with an eleven-year-old boy and having a complaint registered by his mother is heartbreaking. Worse is that the campus police investigation and subsequent reprimand of Sandusky did nothing to stop him from continuing his inappropriate behavior with other young men, according to prosecutors. If anything, it's possible that Sandusky was so relieved that the campus police didn't think his behavior rose to the level of criminality that he became even more emboldened. He also learned that being a prominent figure on campus worked in his favor.

While he was still being investigated for that shower incident, Sandusky spoke at the 1998 commencement ceremonies at State College Area High, which were held in the Bryce Jordan Center of the Penn State campus.

Remarkably two more events of sexual abuse were alleged to have occurred in 2000. The first involved the child who came to the attention of authorities because another child was an eyewitness. The witness said he saw Sandusky inappropriately touching someone from The Second Mile. The child who was allegedly being touched wasn't discovered until Corporal Joe Leiter began his door-to-door investigation nearly ten years later. The young man later told the grand jury that Sandusky had plied him with gifts and trips to football games and other places before he was also taken into the Holuba Hall shower. The physical contact had begun with rubs and hair washes and eventually naked bear hugs, the young man said. Sandusky also invited him to his house for overnights, where Sandusky touched him inappropriately until he'd turn over on his stomach to stop the molestation, he said. The boy stopped all contact with Sandusky, telling his parents he wanted nothing more to do with the man.

By the fall of 2000 Jerry Sandusky was no longer an employee of the university. But he still had an office in the Lasch Building and was authorized to use the sports facilities, workout rooms, and the training centers, along with the changing rooms, saunas, whirlpools, and showers. That fall a janitor named Jim Calhoun told fellow employee Ronald Petrosky that he had witnessed Sandusky performing oral sex on a child who seemed no older than twelve, according to the grand jury report. Petrosky encouraged Calhoun to report what he had witnessed to his supervisor, Jay Witherite. In his testimony before the grand jury, Witherite said he told Calhoun who in the Penn State chain of command to contact if he wanted to report the incident. No report was ever filed by Calhoun, who currently suffers from dementia and is incompetent to testify, according to the grand jury report.

As far as the public was concerned, Sandusky was a model citizen. He received awards and adulation from a number of organizations in 2000. The American Football Coaches Association honored him as the Assistant Coach of the Year at its convention on January 10, 2000. At the presentation ceremony Sandusky spoke on the topic of "Working with Young

People." The Philadelphia Sports Writers Association also honored Sandusky with its career achievement award on January 17, 2000. At another event, this one on April 14, 2000, about 1,200 people attended a testimonial and roasted Sandusky at the Bryce Jordan Center. Joe Paterno made a very brief appearance, saying he had to leave early because of a prior commitment. Paterno said Sandusky was "what Penn State is all about," according to news coverage of the event.

Penn State's first game after Sandusky's retirement was a 24–6 loss to Toledo on September 2, 2000. Sandusky attended the game, but he was not mentioned over the public address system. At Homecoming Weekend on October 21, 2000, Sandusky served as the grand marshal of the homecoming parade. From his seat in an open convertible he tossed candy to the crowd lining the streets.

His coaching days over, Sandusky wrote his life's story in an autobiography. *Touched: the Jerry Sandusky Story* was published in 2001 and detailed the fun times he had working with kids from The Second Mile, including summer camps held on the Penn State campus. In one passage, he wrote, "I believe I live a good part of my life in a make-believe world. I enjoyed pretending as a kid, and I love doing the same as an adult with these kids. Pretending has always been a part of me. I've loved trying to do the right things to hopefully make a difference in kids' lives and maybe make things better off for them . . . I enjoy the life that I have had, and I'll never regret being called a 'great' pretender." In another segment, he wrote: "At the times when I found myself searching for maturity, I usually come up with insanity. That's the way it is in the life of Gerald Arthur Sandusky."

BEHIND THE SCENES HIS CONTACT with Second Mile boys was continuing. Even after the incident in May 2002, when Mike McQueary saw him with a child in the showers, Sandusky still received only minimal punishment. It seemed as though people who could have made certain that law enforcement and child protection became involved chose instead to simply keep Sandusky from bringing kids onto campus. By once again giving him a pass they enforced his sense that he could get away with doing whatever he wanted. Their decision to adhere to Penn State's code of silence rather than sound alarms over the rights and protections of a small child will haunt the campus for a long time. So many elements of the story are distressing, not the least of which is that neither Paterno, nor Curley, nor Schultz, nor McQueary, nor Spanier ever tried to find the boy and get his version of the event. They seemed like they hoped the whole thing would just go away. Banning Sandusky from bringing children onto campus, surrendering his keys, and taking away his privileges seemed to be the best they could come up with. Of course, that had no effect on his behavior. He was still seen at all the football games and freely coming and going from the Lasch Building, where he still had an office. Athletic Director Tim Curley later acknowledged in his grand jury testimony that the ban he imposed on Sandusky was unenforceable. Sandusky continued to use the Penn State facilities for nine more years until he was indicted on November 5, 2011.

On March 28, 2002, Sandusky was a celebrity coach in the annual Easter Bowl, a fundraising football game sponsored by the Easter Seals of Central Pennsylvania. The event raised $14,500 for the Easter Seals. Interestingly, McQueary was one of the players on Sandusky's team for that event.

On April 3, 2003 Sandusky and Katherine Genovese, vice president of programs for The Second Mile, accepted an award on behalf of the charity for Organization of the Year presented by The Pennsylvania School Counselors Association Five months later, Sandusky was presented with a Congressional Angels in Adoption Award after being nominated by the then-U.S. Senator Rick Santorum R-Pennsylvania, a 1980 graduate of Penn State. The citation said: "It is easier to develop a child than rehabilitate an adult."

Despite the supposed restrictions against Sandusky, a twelve-year-old who was attending a Second Mile summer camp at Penn State said he was raped in Sandusky's office in 2004. The young man was not among those who testified before the grand jury, but he filed a lawsuit against Sandusky in 2011. According to the lawsuit, the boy said Sandusky was awarding prizes to Second Milers who could answer questions on current events. The boy was applauded for his correct answer but Sandusky said he had exhausted his supply of prizes. He asked the boy to follow him to his office, where he could find him a gift in his stash. Inside the office, decorated with coaching awards and pictures of kids he had helped through his charity over the years, Sandusky gave the young boy a glass of whiskey and then sexually assaulted him.

"He gets him in a room. He's on one side of the desk, the boy is on other," said his lawyer in a posting on the law firm's website. "[Sandusky] proceeded to engage him in conversation—he had lost his mother, his mother died the year before, he had a very hard time, they were very close—they talked for a while about that. Then [Sandusky] pulled out a glass with alcohol in it and told him to drink it. Then he sodomized him." Afterward Sandusky gave the child a commemorative hockey puck and a bottle inscribed with details of a football championship. The child then returned to The Second Mile camp.

On November 6, 2004, Sandusky was inducted into the Pennsylvania Sports Hall of Fame in Lancaster. His father had been inducted fifteen years earlier.

The following year another boy, this one eleven years old, said he also met Sandusky at a Second Mile camp on the Penn State campus. Sandusky was extremely generous with him, giving him golf clubs, a computer, clothing, and money. He took the boy with him to college and professional sporting events. Then came the invitation for the overnight at the Sanduskys' house. True to the pattern, Sandusky rubbed the boy's back when he was putting him to bed. The contact progressed to Sandusky's performing sex acts on the boy and having the boy engage in similar activity with him, according to testimony given to the investigating grand jury.

Meanwhile, Sandusky and former Penn State players were honored on March 23, 2007, at a fundraiser connected with The Second Mile's Celebration of Excellence program. The event was held in Hershey, Pennsylvania, and was publicized in a news release by the Penn State sport information department. In addition, Sandusky delivered the commencement address on campus for the Penn State College of Health and Human Development on May 19, 2007. Less than a month later, Sandusky participated in a charity golf tournament benefitting The Second Mile. The event involved former football players from Penn State and the University of Pittsburgh.

One of the items sold during a silent auction was as Penn State football jersey autographed by Joe Paterno. In September 2010, Sandusky retired from day-to-day involvement in The Second Mile, saying he wanted to spend more time with his family and to handle personal matters.

The first story about the statewide investigation into Sandusky's alleged sexual abuse of boys in his charity appeared March 31, 2011, in the *Patriot News* of Harrisburg. Penn State's spring practice media day was held the next day, but Joe Paterno, who had testified before the grand jury, refused to answer questions about the story. "Well, I came here to talk about football and this football team, and I don't have any comment on that," Paterno told sports writers.

Sandusky was seen working out at campus facilities a week before he was arrested on November 5, 2011. On the day he was arraigned, the Creamery, the on-campus ice cream factory, still offered a concoction called the Sandusky Blitz, which featured banana-flavored ice cream with chocolate-covered peanuts and caramel swirl.

In an interview published December 3, 2011, in *The New York Times,* Sandusky disputed the notion he had led the double-life of a humanitarian and someone who was sexually assaulting young boys. "They've taken everything that I ever did for any young person and twisted it to say that my motives were sexual or whatever," Sandusky said.

His attorney, Joe Amendola, who sat in on the interview, chimed in. "All those good things you were doing have been turned around, and the people who are painting you as a monster are saying, 'Well, they're the types of things that people who are pedophiles exhibit, ' " Amendola told the newspaper.

Four days after that interview was published, Sandusky was arrested and arraigned on new charges brought by two new accusers, bringing the total number to ten young men who had told their stories under oath to an investigating grand jury. One young man, identified by prosecutors as Victim 9, said he was sexually assaulted after meeting Sandusky in 1997. Another, listed in the indictment as Victim 10, said the sex abuse by Sandusky started in 2004.

"As in many of the other cases identified to date, the contact with Sandusky allegedly fit a pattern of grooming victims," Attorney General Linda Kelly said in a statement on December 7, 2011. "Beginning with outings to football games and gifts, they later included physical contact that escalated to sexual assaults."

At his second arraignment, Sandusky befittingly wore a blue-and-white Penn State workout outfit with a Nittany Lion logo.

CHAPTER FIFTEEN

———

PRELIMINARY HEARING FOR CURLEY AND SCHULTZ

On December 16, 2011, Tim Curley and Gary Schultz solemnly emerged from their vehicles at the Dauphin County Courthouse in Harrisburg after their eighty-mile drive from State College. As police officers held back the crowd, the men and their lawyers entered the mammoth stone courthouse through the main doors on Market and Front Streets. They passed through metal detectors and then were screened with electronic wands by guards stationed just outside the courtroom doors. The public was about to hear testimony for the first time related to the child sex abuse charges brought against Jerry Sandusky.

Both men were facing a preliminary hearing on charges that they failed to act properly in a 2002 incident on campus involving Sandusky and a ten-year-old boy, and that they had lied about it before a statewide investigative grand jury. The media had gathered to witness the public proceedings, but the number of reporters was half the throng that had gathered three days

GAME OVER

earlier in Bellefonte at the Centre County Courthouse. Even though their ranks had been thinned, media members and other courtroom observers who were granted seats through a lottery system had to wait in a long queue to enter the courthouse. They too had to file past the menacing police dogs and through the double layer of security to get inside the proceedings presided over by District Judge William C. Wenner.

Before the hearing convened, a court administrator warned everyone in the crowded room that no outbursts would be tolerated and that anyone who left during the proceeding would not be allowed to return until a recess was called. Those inside the room were told to remain seated at all times, even if a fire alarm sounded. These rules were to prevent distractions in the spacious chamber, even though the judge earlier had granted permission to reporters to bring their laptops inside so that they could transmit accounts of the hearing to social media networks.

Just before nine o'clock Curley and Schultz settled into their seats. In front of them was a marble wall on which were chiseled the words "No man can be deprived of his life, liberty or property unless by the judgment of his peers or by the law of the land." The fate of Curley and Schultz hinged largely on the testimony of another Penn State employee, Mike McQueary. The lawyers for Curley and Schultz steadfastly contended they had not committed any crimes, but the attorneys also knew that the preliminary hearing would likely result in a ruling that would send the case to a full trial.

In the preliminary hearing the prosecution's burden was only to show that there was reasonable suspicion that a crime had been committed. Once that evidentiary hurdle was cleared, the cases would go to trial. No one expected the men to waive their hearing as Sandusky had done, or that the charges against them would be dropped. The Pennsylvania attorney general had publicly announced that McQueary had already told a grand jury what he had witnessed. Still, anticipation was palpable in the courtroom.

The government's case was built on what McQueary said he told Curley and Schultz about the nature of the incident and what the two Penn State officials had sworn was the truth before the grand jury. McQueary claimed he had reported a very specific sexual assault to them. Both Curley and

Schultz said the assistant coach mentioned inappropriate horseplay, but not a sexual assault.

At eight minutes after nine o'clock the lawyers for Curley and Schultz waived the reading of the indictments against them. Next McQueary walked quickly through the chamber's back door and up the room's center aisle past both defendants to the witness box. Dressed in a blue pinstriped suit, he raised his right hand and swore that what he was about to say was the truth.

After taking his seat McQueary nodded toward Curley. He rubbed his ears and the tightly shorn sides of his bright red hair before he consumed the first of many cups of water he would down during the next two hours of testimony. A helpless frown had replaced the broad smile friends were accustomed to seeing on Curley's face as McQueary began. Schultz, sitting at semi-attention on the edge of his chair, alternately gazed at McQueary and at the legal notebook in front of him.

In a deliberate tone, McQueary repeated what he had said before the grand jury. He happened upon Sandusky and the child after venturing to the Lasch Building at nine o'clock on a Friday night before the beginning of spring break 2002 to retrieve films of potential Penn State recruits. He went to the graduate assistant locker room to put away a pair of new sneakers when he heard the slapping sounds of wet skin from what could have been a sex act. As he walked toward the shower he saw through a reflection in a mirror Sandusky leaning against a child. On a second trip into the area seconds later, he witnessed Sandusky holding the child's waist from behind, their bodies locked together. He retreated again, slammed the door of his locker shut, and returned for a third view. By then the man and the boy had separated. He didn't see Sandusky's genitalia or penetration, he said, but added, "That's what I believe was happening," especially since he saw the boy's hands against the shower wall. Once he saw them apart, he thought the child was safe and figured it was best to leave the awkward situation because his mind was racing. "To be frank, I can't describe what I was feeling or thinking. Shocked and horrified, quite frankly, not thinking straight. I was distraught," McQueary said from the witness chair.

Caroline Roberto, Curley's lawyer, focused on details during her cross-examination. But McQueary stuck to his story in a matter-of-fact voice. He couldn't be 100 percent certain it was a rape, he told Roberto. "But I'm sure I saw what I saw."

"Did you say anything to Sandusky?" Roberto asked.

"No, nothing," he responded.

"You didn't confront him at all over what you saw?"

"They looked directly at me," he said.

"What was the expression?"

"A somewhat blank expression."

Roberto asked McQueary why he didn't notify authorities. "Did you consider calling the police?"

"Absolutely . . . without a doubt," McQueary said.

"Did you?"

"No, I did not call police."

Attorney Thomas Farrell of Pittsburgh, who represented Schultz, later delved into the details of what McQueary said he saw. He challenged whether or not Sandusky, who at six-feet-two-inches tall, could have sex with a short-statured child in the physical position described without lifting him off the ground. He wondered if McQueary's view of whatever was going on would have been obstructed by the former coach's body. He also got McQueary to admit he did not know what color the child's hair was or other details normally associated with credible eyewitness accounts.

Preliminary hearings limited cross-examination on any topic not broached by the prosecutors first, so defense lawyers were unable to challenge McQueary about such details as the design of the locker room or the size of the shower. McQueary did say he was so unnerved, he dashed to his second-floor office and phoned his father. "I said, I just saw Coach Sandusky in the showers with a boy, what I saw was wrong and sexual, and I needed some advice quickly," he testified.

His father told him to come to his house in State College, where a family friend, Dr. Jonathan Dranov, joined them for the discussion. The three of them decided to forgo calling the police, but to have McQueary report the scene to Joe Paterno. McQueary said he took the advice, and the following morning went to Paterno's house. "I saw Jerry with a young boy in the shower and it was way over the lines, extremely sexual in nature and I thought I needed to tell him about it."

Out of respect for Paterno, who was seventy-eight at the time, he did not reveal the graphic details of what he saw. But he was sure from the coach's reaction that he knew the context of the act.

Bruce Beemer, a deputy attorney general, handled the questioning. "Did you make it clear it was Jerry Sandusky?" he queried.

"Yes, I did," replied McQueary.

"Did you make it clear it was a young boy?"

"Yes, I did."

"Did you make it clear it was sexual?"

"Without a doubt."

McQueary said Paterno was shocked and saddened. The coach professed sorrow that his graduate assistant had to witness such a thing, but told him he'd done the right thing. He said he'd report it to the proper authorities.

The "proper authority" Paterno would seek out was Tim Curley. Paterno had watched him grow from a Penn State football player to a low-level aid in the Penn State Athletic Department to the school's athletic director, hand-picked for the job by JoePa himself. Paterno told Curley about McQueary's shocking allegation, and Curley said he'd relay the report to Schultz.

At issue from the time Paterno and Curley first spoke and throughout the entire investigation of the Penn State officials was the exact nature and substance of the complaints against Sandusky. While Paterno and Mc-Queary and later McQueary's father would claim the young coach always described the incident as a sexual assault, Curley would swear that neither Paterno nor McQueary ever mentioned sexual contact. Schultz backed up Curley's statements.

Neither Curley nor Schultz testified at the preliminary hearing. Paterno, hospitalized with a broken hip and under treatment for lung cancer, was not available to take the stand either. Instead the testimony of all three men was read into the court record.

"He [McQueary] said he saw a mature person, fondling, whatever you might call it, I'm not sure what the term would be . . . a young boy," Paterno

said in testimony delivered to the grand jury on January 12, 2011. "It was
of a sexual nature, I'm not sure exactly what it was and didn't push Mike to
describe it." Paterno also testified that his involvement ended after Curley,
a man he trusted implicitly, told him he would handle it.

McQueary said it was not until nine or ten days later that he was
summoned to a meeting with Curley and Schultz. "I told them I saw Jerry
Sandusky in the showers with a young boy in what seemed was extremely
sexual, over the lines and it was wrong," McQueary said. Under questioning by Beemer, he testified that he told the two officials about the sounds
he heard in the shower and the body positions of Sandusky and the boy. "I
would have described them as extremely sexual and that some sort of intercourse was going on." Asked specifically if he told the officials that Sandusky was committing a sexual act against the child, McQueary answered,
"There is no doubt at all."

If Curley and Schultz had simply said that McQueary told them the
event he witnessed in the shower was sexual in nature, they probably would
never have been charged with perjury, leaving the case with only the "failure to report" count, which Curley's lawyer insultingly compared to a traffic ticket. But if he had conceded to what the prosecutors were pushing,
Curley essentially would have had to admit an eight-year cover-up of the
2002 event. Curley claimed he did not make those admissions because they
were not true.

Curley's grand jury testimony, read into the record at the preliminary
hearing, was as emphatic as it was contradictory to the testimony of others.
"My recollection was there were people in the shower area, horsing around,
playful, but it was not appropriate," he testified. He had been questioned repeatedly by Frank Fina, head of the attorney general's investigations branch,
at the grand jury. Curley insisted that McCreary never told him the event
amounted to a sexual assault. Because there hadn't been any indication of
criminality, he called McQueary to tell him he had taken action with the
full blessing of Schultz and Graham Spanier, the university's president.

In Spanier's testimony before the grand jury the previous April he
stated that neither of his underlings had told him about the sexual nature
of the report. Nevertheless Sandusky did suffer repercussions. The Second

Mile's CEO, John Raykovitz, was informed of the incident so he could take his own action. As far as Penn State was concerned, Sandusky was ordered not to bring kids around the football program or its facilities at any point in the future and to forfeit his keys to the facilities. The grand jury testimony stated that Paterno told McQueary what actions had been taken and asked if the actions were acceptable to him.

"I accepted what he told me and said 'okay,'" McQueary testified.

Curley said he spoke with Schultz repeatedly about the issue. He explained why no criminal referral or complaint was filed with police or other agencies: "I didn't think it was a crime at the time." Neither he nor anyone in power at Penn State sought to determine the identity of the child. While his testimony matched Curley's, Schultz admitted he was one of the few Penn State officials who knew about the allegations of child abuse leveled against Sandusky in 1998. Once the district attorney, Ray Gricar, decided not to pursue charges against Sandusky and the state welfare investigators considered the allegations of abuse unfounded, that probe was hushed up too. Gricar was declared legally dead in July 2011, six years after he disappeared without a trace forty-five miles east of State College. The missing persons investigation is ongoing; some people speculate that the disappearance is somehow tied to the Sandusky case. It would be irresponsible not to note that the week before Gricar disappeared he had very publicly announced the largest heroin bust in Centre County's history, an event that undoubtedly earned him lots of dangerous enemies.

Mike's father, John McQueary, took the stand at the preliminary hearing to testify about two events. Deputy District Attorney Bruce Beemer handled his questioning too. First, the elder McQueary testified to the conversation he had with his son the night the young man witnessed the assault. Next he testified about a conversation he had with Schultz during an unrelated business meeting a few months later. The elder McQueary said he told Schultz the issues surrounding Sandusky were important, "and that there should be something done about it."

"Did you refer to Sandusky?" asked Beemer.

"Absolutely, yes."

"Did you describe the nature of the incident?"

"Yes."

"What words did you use?"

The elder McQueary said he related to Schultz that his son told him he "saw Jerry Sandusky in the shower with a young boy and that between the sounds . . . and the visualization . . . there was something at best that was inappropriate, and it was sexual in nature."

John McQueary said Schultz told him he had heard things about Sandusky before, apparently referring to the 1998 event. "What he indicated was that they had heard allegations and were aware of the situation, and they would look into it." He testified that Schultz told him they'd looked at similar reports before, but "he was never able to sink their teeth into something that was substantial. . . . But I got the impression he was going to look at it more." McQueary said he was disappointed that nothing came of this.

During the preliminary hearing Thomas R. Harmon, director of the campus police from 1992 to 2005, said he was never told about McQueary's allegations against Sandusky. He knew about the 1998 incident because the investigation was conducted by his police force, but he defended the outcome as proper because there was no specific evidence "of touching of genitals or anything overtly sexual about this incident," a statement both the child and his mother would contest. What Harmon did not tell the grand jury or defense lawyers inquiring about his actions was that he and Sandusky were former neighbors. The two families had lived in the same community for several years dating back to 1977, the year the coach started The Second Mile. Their children had played together in the Norle Street cul-de-sac until the Sanduskys moved to a bigger house two miles away in 1984. The Sandusky and Harmon families also attended the same church.

For his part, Gary Schultz's sworn grand jury testimony, entered into the record, also denied that McQueary or anyone else specified any criminal behavior. "I had the feeling there was some kind of wrestling-around activity and maybe Jerry might have grabbed the young boy's genitals," Schultz said. He admitted that any such conduct was clearly inappropriate but said, "The allegations came across as not that serious," and certainly didn't rise to illegal behavior. "There was no indication that it was." To reinforce his point of view, Schultz said he believed a central Pennsylvania social services agency was told about it. He just couldn't remember which one it was.

Anthony Sassano, an investigator for the attorney general's office, testified before Judge Wenner that no regional police or social service agencies under subpoena produced even one report about complaints made to them regarding the McQueary allegations. Schultz had responded with surprise. "Wow, I thought it was turned over," he had told the grand jury months earlier.

In 2011 at least six more young men would go before that same panel to claim abuse at Sandusky's hand.

Within a year of reporting the incident, Mike McQueary was appointed as a full-time assistant coach for the Nittany Lions football team. McQueary would have no further discussions with law enforcement until October 2010. That's when state police and investigators for the attorney general's office contacted him.

As expected, when all the testimony was concluded, Curley and Schultz were held for trial. Senior Deputy Attorney General Marc Costanzo told reporters the preliminary hearing offered a brief taste of what was to come at trial, which was not expected to be held until late 2012 at the earliest. Costanzo said prosecutors would present further evidence showing the extent of the Penn State cover-up the two defendants helped perpetrate and then lied about. The stakes were high.

Penn State is footing the legal bills for Curley and Schultz, its two employees. If convicted, Curley would lose his coveted job but because he invested his retirement savings in a private mutual fund account, he will be able to keep his money, no matter what the outcome. Schultz is at risk of losing his retirement savings if convicted; his $5 million is invested in the state's retirement system. A forfeiture provision holds that state officials convicted of crimes, such as job-related perjury, can lose all benefits. In Schultz's case, this amounts to retirement fund payments of almost $28,000 a month.

After the preliminary hearing both Caroline Roberto and Thomas Farrell, the lawyers for Curley and Schultz, respectively, again admonished the attorney general's office for even bringing the cases against their clients. Roberto said the government did not provide evidence of the single most important element of perjury under Pennsylvania law: corroboration. One of the few people who could have corroborated the testimony was no longer available to do so.

CHAPTER SIXTEEN

———

PENN STATE'S REPUTATION

There is a count that puts the number of living Penn State alumni at more than 560,000 worldwide. James F. Murtha, fifty-seven, was proud to be one of them. He graduated from Penn State in 1977 with a degree in journalism and once covered Penn State football games. His wife, Lisa, was a Penn Stater. Some of his best friends were alums with season tickets to football games. He was angry and dismayed about the damage done to Penn State's reputation in the fallout from the arrests and how the university's administration handled it and reacted to it.

Murtha was attending a conference of the Independent Oil and Gas Association in mid-November 2011 in upstate New York. As a legislative affairs consultant, his responsibilities were to provide information to local officials about the impact on water wells from drilling into the Marcellus Shale rock formation and extracting an energy source through a process called hydraulic fracturing, or fracking. During the presentations Murtha listened intently as a geologist used charts and graphs to explain the procedure. When the geologist referred to a cutting-edge study on environmental concerns done by Penn State University, his alma mater, he tensed up.

"He said this study comes from Penn State, so please, no laughing. And there was some snickering in the audience because this was when Jerry Sandusky was all over the news," Murtha said. "It was the first time in my life I ever heard Penn State mentioned in the context of a joke. It really bothered me.

"I have a ton of affection for that place. I really enjoyed my four years there. I got a good education that prepared me for life. And now we've all been tarred with the same brush. We have to make apologies for an entire school because of what a retired football coach did. I couldn't feel any worse if somebody shot my dog. It really pisses me off. But in retrospect, you could almost predict how this would turn out because of the way Penn State does business. Isolation is one of its charms, but it's also part of the problem. They all drank the Kool-Aid up there. They lost all focus. The only way to solve a problem is to admit that you have one. It's crisis management 101. When I saw the way they handled it, I wanted to projectile vomit."

The inner conflict of love for a university and disgust over a child sex abuse scandal was something that Penn State's 560,000 alumni were wrestling with, each in his or her own way. But Murtha, for one, was not blaming outside forces for causing the damage. What bothered him most were the missed opportunities to stop the abuse, particularly the 1998 investigation by campus police that went nowhere and the 2002 incident witnessed by Mike McQueary. "Penn State administrators are people who were intelligent enough to run a multibillion dollar operation and sophisticated enough to deal with any problem. Yet every time they had an opportunity to make the right decision, they did the wrong thing. To me, the attitude seems to have been to circle the wagons, to protect the brand at all costs. A child abuse scandal would go against the narrative they tried to write. Kids' lives were destroyed. No brand is worth the lives of ten-year-old boys."

It will take more time to sift through the rubble to determine who knew what and when they knew it, Murtha said. The impact on Joe Paterno's legacy will hinge on what McQueary told the legendary coach and what Paterno reported up the chain of command. What's haunting, however, are Paterno's own words—that he wished he would have done more—after Sandusky was charged with fifty-two counts of sexually assaulting ten boys from The Second Mile over a fifteen-year period.

"You can't argue that Joe succeeded in winning football games with players who had to go to class," Murtha said. "I was proud of the fact that Penn State was never investigated for recruiting violations or cheating. I was proud of the high graduation rates. Joe did do things the right way. But in his own words, his sin was one of omission, a lapse in judgment. Just follow the thread. McQueary goes to his dad and then goes to Joe. JoePa doesn't have a badge. He's not a cop. Then JoePa reports it to his superiors, but he had no superiors. Nobody on that campus told him what to do. For decades, JoePa was the center of attention in every room he walked into. Getting an interview with him was like getting an interview with the pope. It's just going to take a lot of time for the whole story to come out. I do a lot of business all over the country. Somebody told me that the Penn State people are no longer virgins, that now they're whores like everybody else. I don't even know how to respond to that right now."

If Penn State football was about success on the field and in the classroom, Penn State University had always been more than a football program. Through the years it had accumulated a lengthy list of renowned graduates. It was the school of Hugh Ellsworth Rodham and Hugh Edwin Rodham, the father and brother of Secretary of State Hillary Rodham Clinton. Penn State educated Lieutenant Michael Murphy, an honors student in political science and psychology who was posthumously awarded the Medal of Honor for fighting in Afghanistan as a member of the Navy SEALs. Valerie Plame, the former CIA officer who wrote the book *My Betrayal by the White House,* was an alumna of Penn State.

Seventeen graduates of Penn State became presidents of colleges and universities. Among the alumni were three former or current U.S. senators and four U.S. congressmen. Tom Ridge, a former governor of Pennsylvania and the first secretary of the Department of Homeland Security, went to Penn State and frequented the Paterno home for Sue Paterno's dinners after football games.

Penn Staters made their mark in the business world as well. One alumnus was Frank Smeal, a partner in the Wall Street firm of Goldman Sachs, whose name is attached to the school's Smeal College of Business. Patricia A. Woertz of Archer Daniels Midland was named to *Fortune* magazine's list of most powerful women in business. Her fellow Penn Staters include William Schreyer, chairman emeritus and former CEO of Merrill Lynch; Louis D'Ambrosio, CEO of Sears Holdings Corp.; Richard A. Zimmerman, CEO of Hershey Foods Corp.; Tom Clarke and Mark Parker, CEOs of Nike Inc.; Steve Sheetz of Sheetz Inc., an Altoona-based chain of gas stations and convenience stores; Joel N. Myers, founder and CEO of AccuWeather; and Kathleen Casey, commissioner of the U.S. Securities and Exchange Commission. What's more, Penn State produced the labor leader Richard Trumka, president of the AFL-CIO.

Scientists came from Penn State. Paul Berg was awarded the 1980 Nobel Prize in Chemistry. Erwin Wilhelm Muller, inventor of the ion microscope, was the first person to see an atom. John Almquist won a Wolf Foundation Award in 1981 for his work on the artificial insemination of dairy cattle. Guion Buford, the first African American in space, attended Penn State. So did fellow astronauts Robert Cenker, James Pawelczyk, and Paul Weitz.

Penn State graduates also contributed to bringing fun to the world. Herman Fisher was a cofounder of the Fisher-Price toy company, and Richard T. James invented the Slinky, the official toy of Pennsylvania.

The university provided a college education to John Aniston, the actor and father of Jennifer Aniston; Jonathan Frakes, an actor and the director of *Star Trek: The Next Generation;* and Benjy Bronk, a comedian and writer for *The Howard Stern Show.*

Writers who attended the school include Julius Epstein, the screenwriter of *Casablanca;* David B. Morrell, author of *First Blood,* the book that inspired the movie character John Rambo; and Richard Russo, the Pulitzer Prize-winning author of *Empire Falls.* Margaret Carlson, the first female columnist for *Time,* graduated from Penn State. So did Norman Miller, a Pulitzer Prize-winning journalist and former chief of the *Wall Street Journal's* Washington bureau, and Tom Verducci, a senior writer for *Sports Illustrated.* Penn State's School of Journalism taught the basic skills of professional reporting to Sara Ganim. Working as a reporter for the *Patriot News* in Harrisburg, Ganim first broke the news of the Jerry Sandusky investigation in a story on March 31, 2011. She reported that a statewide grand jury was looking into allegations that Sandusky had indecently assaulted a teenage boy.

But a cloud hangs over everything Penn State these days. "Heartbreaking" is the word used by Charles Pittman, the first African American recruited by Joe Paterno to play football at Penn State and the man who sent his son, Tony, to play for JoePa. The Pittmans wrote the book *Playing for Paterno,* published by Triumph Books in 2007. In it they describe how they applied the lessons they learned from Paterno to the business world. As a newspaper executive for Schurz Communications and a member of the board of directors for the Associated Press, Pittman has struggled to process the raw hurt resulting from a child sex abuse scandal that caused the fall of a coach who was a father figure and brought disgrace to the school he loves so much.

"It's like a death in the family," said Pittman. "I was defined by Penn State football and the Joe Paterno Way. I bought into the concepts of trust and loyalty and respect, that it's important to win, but it's more important to prepare for how you approach life. I taught my son those same concepts. In my professional career, I managed people in the business world with those concepts. It's the way I lived my life."

Pittman was in private contact with Paterno through letters and phone calls after the coach was fired. He has not given interviews and doesn't pretend to speak for other alumni, but when asked, he spoke from his broken heart about his shock and anger and something much, much deeper—the distressing feelings of embarrassment and shame.

As for Jerry Sandusky, Pittman said simply, "He deceived us."

His thoughts of Paterno are more complex. "Was I hoodwinked?" Pittman asked himself rhetorically. "I don't think I was hoodwinked. I've always known him to be a genuine person. I bought into what he was saying, and it worked for me. I like to think I have Pittman family values, but Joe shaped them and made them better. I think he got trapped by his own success. It's like a Greek tragedy. I don't want to presuppose anything because most of the story has yet to come out. But Joe didn't have a boss at Penn State. He hand-picked his own boss in Tim Curley. It got to a point where people didn't question him. Absolute power corrupts absolutely. I'm not saying he was corrupt, but the power he created provided the opportunity for corruption to breed. That's what makes this so mind-boggling.

"People love to tear down icons in America. They love to see the mighty fall. They can't wait to see them fail. After all that Joe accomplished, he will also be remembered for saying that he wished he would have done more. O. J. Simpson, Richard Nixon, Pete Rose, Bill Clinton, Barry Bonds, Tiger Woods—they are all remembered for their last, worst act. I try to live my life remembering that one bad act can destroy everything I've built, and that it's better to leave too soon than to stay too long. That's why I'm heartbroken."

To Pittman, football was not a game of knocking people down; it was about helping people back up. In his understanding of the Grand Experiment, it was important to win but it was more important to prepare for life outside the football arena. After the 1999 football season Pittman was invited back to Penn State to speak at the banquet honoring the senior players. Too shy to sing when he arrived on campus thirty-three years earlier, he eloquently sang the praises of the school he attended. "I used to tell people that I did more for Penn State than Penn State did for me. I was wrong. Penn State did more for me than I could ever do for Penn State," Pittman told his audience. "Joe always said that people would ask him which of his football teams was the greatest. He would answer to ask him in twenty years, after his last team played, so he could see how many CEOs, teachers, doctors, lawyers and elected leaders were on that team."

Gregory White, a senior manager at CommVault in Austin, Texas, was particularly upset about the riots in State College following Paterno's dismissal. He interpreted that support for JoePa as support for pedophilia. He wrote in a letter to the editor of the *Daily Collegian* at Penn State dated November 15, 2011, that said, "I have had my corporation's staff working this holiday weekend to go through all employee files. Anyone who went to Penn State will have their final checks waiting for them Monday morning and no

one from Penn State will ever be hired by any company I run in the future."
This was an example of just how far-reaching the scandal had become.

Even students who collect money for charity have been vilified. Penn
State is known for having the largest student-run philanthropy in the world.
Since 1977 students have raised $78 million for The Four Diamonds Fund,
supporting Penn State Hershey Children's Hospital. But when a first-year
student, Holly Semanchick, was out collecting money for the fund in Beth-
lehem, Pennsylvania, on the first weekend of December 2011, a driver in a
passing car spit at her.

"All the faith is now being questioned. People are trying to invalidate
what was validated," Pittman said. "We can't undo what happened. And we
can't undo what Penn State stands for and what it represents. We are not
defined by the school we attend or how many football games we win, but
how we perform and take advantage of our opportunities. If a guy says he
won't hire a Penn State graduate, I don't want to work for that guy anyway.
It's going to take time. We don't know the full story yet. But we should not
be deterred by these events. It was a few people who failed to do what they
should have done. Why should what happened diminish what any of us
stands for?"

Gary Gray, an investment banker and a visiting professor of finance
in the Smeal College of Business, is among those Penn State alumni who
don't believe the university engaged in a whitewash. A three-year letterman in football from 1969 to 1971, he was coached by Jerry Sandusky and
played racquetball with him once a week. "The thing that bothers me is the
accusation of a cover-up," said Gray. "It doesn't make any sense. There's no
cover-up. No one thought anything of this nature was probable or even possible. I still can't believe any of this.

"The Jerry I know is an all-around good guy. Nobody thought he was
capable of doing anything like he's accused of. But it almost doesn't matter
if he is or isn't. The fallout has happened. People are embarrassed to say
they went to Penn State. It's just sad. I understand that there are ten young
men beating the same drum, saying the same things. My personal view is,
if this occurred—and let's not forget the justice system has to play itself

out—it's the act of one person. You can't condemn an entire university for it."

Some white-hot anger has been directed at the thirty-two members of Penn State's board of trustees. The board has become a target for not knowing more about the investigation, for firing Joe Paterno, and for the late-night phone call during which Paterno was fired.

A group called Penn Staters for Responsible Stewardship has held a series of meetings around the state to call attention to their belief that Joe Paterno was denied due process before he was fired by the board of trustees on November 9, 2011. The leaders of this group are Anthony Lubrano, a 1982 graduate of Penn State's Smeal College of Business, and Franco Harris, a Penn State football player who had a Hall of Fame professional career with the Pittsburgh Steelers. They say their message is not about guilt or innocence, but that everyone is innocent until proven guilty. "The university responded inappropriately to the situation. Their response set us down a path that has harmed our reputation," Lubrano said.

Harris has been outspoken from the start about the board of trustees. "We cannot let them write this last chapter. We have to keep fighting for Penn State," he said. The night of Paterno's firing, Harris said, he sent a text message to one of the trustees that said, "You guys are a bunch of wimps."

FOUR GENERATIONS OF ANNE RILEY'S family have gone to Penn State. Her father, Ridge Riley, a sports journalist and longtime president of the Penn State Alumni Association, was the creator and author of the Association's *Football Letter*, a two-sided, single-sheet letter filled with highlights and photos of every Saturday game. Ridge worked on the *Football Letter* for thirty-eight years. One of the honors Penn State bestows on a football player at the conclusion of every season is the Ridge Riley Award, named for the man everyone knew as "Mr. Penn State." Every Sunday during football season Ridge would show up at Paterno's house and talk football with the coach around his kitchen table. On his last visit, in January 1976, he asked, "How do we stand right now, right here, with the football program?" Before he could get JoePa's answer, he put his head down on the table, saying he didn't feel well. He had suffered a fatal heart attack. Paterno held him in his arms until the ambulance responding to the 911 call arrived.

Anne Riley met Paterno when she was only eight years old. She grew up in the State College area, graduated from Penn State with a degree in liberal arts, taught English at State College High School, and in her conversations with Paterno they discussed opera and Virgil's poetry. In her father's book, *Road to Number One: A Personal Chronicle of Penn State Football*, published posthumously by Doubleday, the coach quoted Virgil's *Aeneid*. "Of arms and the man I sing," he wrote to his dear friend in the book's introduction.

Anne Riley serves on the Penn State board of trustees, just as her father did. During an agonizing night, November 9, 2011, she voted in favor of firing Joe Paterno. "It took everything I had," Riley said two months after casting that vote. "I won't tell you why. But I've lived here all my life. To me, Penn State and State College are inseparable. I taught at State College High School, my mother's high school. I taught the children of Penn State. I thought of them as my children. Children are number one with me. That's why we're here as educators. So I can tell you the night the trustees voted, we did what we had to do." It was the thought of the young men who said under oath that they had been abused by Jerry Sandusky and the thought of tomorrow's children that influenced her thought process.

"We aren't past this crisis yet. We have to let it all play out in the courts," Riley said. "But collectively, we need to get on with our work. I want us to be reminded of the true purpose of this school. Because of our situation, our place in this terrible story, I want us to do everything we can to do better at caring for our children. We want to be a leader in the cause of caring for our children. If that is what it means to come out of the ashes, we are ready to lead. The desire to lead has never been so strong. We must get to the truth."

She said the board of trustees has no desire to belittle the achievements of Graham Spanier and Joe Paterno. Indeed she wants to trumpet the good that they stand for, even as she wrestles with the anguish that much of the child molestation allegedly took place on the Penn State campus. "All of us in our own way will be forever sorrowful it had to happen this way. We aren't past this yet. The anger will continue. I would hope the friendships do too."

In early December 2011 Penn State announced it would donate $1.5 million to a partnership it had entered into with the Pennsylvania Co-alition Against Rape and the National Sexual Violence Resource Center. In addition, the university is pledging at least $500,000 to create the Center for the Protection of Children at the Penn State Hershey Children's Hospi-tal. It is hoped the new center will become the home of national experts on child abuse. "We have committed ourselves to being the national leader on the prevention and treatment of child abuse, so that we will have a mean-ingful role in fighting this horrific crime," the university's president Rodney Erickson said in a news release announcing the creation of the center. The money for the partnership and the center comes from the football bowl revenues Penn State receives from the Big Ten Conference.

But however the university sought to define itself in the aftermath of the Sandusky scandal, it would have to move forward without Joe Paterno, the football coach who had become the face of Penn State.

CHAPTER SEVENTEEN

A COACH'S FAREWELL

Many of the sidewalks in the business district and residential neighborhoods of State College were still covered with the seven inches of snow from a late January storm that blanketed the campus and the nearby landmark of Mount Nittany. A single set of boot prints led to the bronze image of an iconic coach who had been fired over the phone two and a half months earlier. The dormant stadium was eerily quiet, a stark contrast to the noise made by 106,000 fanatics on football Saturdays. Then word spread across campus and around town that Paterno, fighting for his life at Mount Nittany Medical Center, had reached the doors of death.

His family had been summoned to the bedside of the eighty-five-year-old patriarch, who had been weakened by treatments for lung cancer as he recovered from a broken hip. Rather than holding a vigil at the hospital, friends and fans made their way to the statue. A student wielding a borrowed shovel scraped the snow away from the base. More well-wishers, drawn like pilgrims to a shrine, lit candles. Some new arrivals brought personal items and laid them at the statue's base. Roses, hats, pennants, pompoms, and a striped blue necktie with the Nittany Lion logo lay among the candles flickering in the winter wind. One offering was a folded T-shirt emblazoned with one of Paterno's favorite sayings: "Believe in Your Heart You Are Destined to Do Great Things."

Activity increased on Sunday morning, January 22, 2012. One man made the hour-long drive from Lewisburg to leave a framed picture of the coach in rolled-up trouser cuffs showing white socks and black shoes. Another fan, his frosty breath visible, wiped a tear from his cheek as he stood quietly. A woman made the sign of the cross and caressed her rosary beads. A satellite TV truck, the vanguard of many more to come, found a parking spot along the curb.

Shortly before ten o'clock Kim Gasper of nearby Bellefonte walked from a snow-covered parking lot toward the statue, carrying her son, Jonathan. She wore a Penn State parka but had never gone to Penn State. Her twenty-month-old toddler wore tiny sneakers adorned with the Nittany Lion logo. Standing next to the statue, she whispered into her son's ear, and the toddler added his tribute, a tiny stuffed lion cub, to the growing collection of items. In that moment the silent gesture spoke louder than a noisy stadium crowd ever could.

Gasper, a special education teacher, felt compelled to visit the statue. Some thirty-five years earlier she had been an eighth grade student in Hazelton, Pennsylvania, who was given a class assignment to write a letter to someone she admired. She chose Joe Paterno. And to her amazement, the coach wrote back, and they continued a correspondence through the years. When she heard JoePa's condition had worsened, she reread some of his letters. One encouraged her to study hard; another cheered her commitment to run in her first marathon. She had once met the coach in person, and Sue Paterno, the coach's wife, came to visit her in the hospital when Jonathon was born. To Gasper, Paterno did more than coach football players. He provided inspiration to little girls nurturing dreams of their own.

"He meant so much to me," said Gasper, sobbing gently. "You know it's going to happen to all of us some time, but when the end comes, it hurts."

Just moments after Gasper left for home in a sport utility vehicle adorned with lion's paw decals, word officially came that Joseph Vincent Paterno had passed away at twenty-five minutes after nine o'clock. His death came sixty-five days after his family announced he was being treated for lung cancer, and seventy-four days after he was fired in the fallout from the Jerry Sandusky scandal. In his final moments Paterno had the opportunity to say goodbye to his wife, his five children, and his seventeen grandchildren in his hospital room. The Paterno family issued a statement: "He fought hard until the end, stayed positive, thought only of others and constantly reminded everyone of how blessed his life had been."

Police blocked off the entrance to McKee Street to discourage mourners from descending on the Paterno home. There was nothing but stillness at the stone-and-glass home at 830 McKee Street. A single sign on the snow-covered lawn read, "We Love You JoePa."

Reaction to his death came from everywhere. One of the first statements read, "He maintained a high standard in a very difficult profession. Joe preached toughness, hard work and clean competition. Most importantly, he had the courage to practice what he preached." It came, jarringly, from Jerry Sandusky, confined to his home in State College by an electronic monitor as a condition of bail. It had been thirteen years since Sandusky resigned from Paterno's coaching staff. What Paterno did or didn't do after first learning of Sandusky's conduct had led to his departure as head coach.

A solemn mood descended over all of central Pennsylvania as word spread of Paterno's death, which inexplicably had been announced prematurely on some websites. Four days of mourning would follow for a father figure who had come to Penn State sixty-one years earlier and had been head coach of a storied program for forty-six years, longer than any college football coach had served at any one school. Flags flying over state office buildings were lowered to half-staff by the executive order of Governor Tom Corbett, who had begun the Sandusky investigation as the state's attorney general. As governor Corbett served as an ex-officio member of the Penn State board of trustees and had supported Paterno's firing.

Hundreds of football players who had been coached by Paterno made their way back to State College to honor their mentor. Among them was Shane Conlan, who was a freshman linebacker when Paterno won his first national championship in 1982 and who was captain of the 1986 national championship team. A native of Frewsburg, New York, who now resides in Pittsburgh, Conlan was a two-time All-American at Penn State and was an All-Pro three times in a professional football career with the Buffalo Bills and St. Louis Rams. Conlan and a former Penn State teammate, Dan Delligatti, had visited Paterno a week after the coach was fired. They sat around Paterno's kitchen table, the gathering place for so many eventful sessions over the years, and talked about life.

"It was a tough time for him, but the first thing he asked about was our families and our kids. He remembered my parents by their first names," said Conlan, vice president of Esmark Inc. "People have said that he died of a broken heart. Not in my view. He was too tough for that. He was too much of a fighter. He wanted to have a press conference to tell his story, but his health wouldn't let him. One of the last things he said was that he was very demanding of us—maybe too demanding—but I didn't want to hear that. I've known from day one that he was not so much about X's and O's as a football coach but more about making sure we graduated and molding us as men. He wasn't coaching us for professional football, he was preparing us for life. He took eighteen-year-old boys and turned us into men. Outside of my father, he had more influence on my life than any other man. I gave him a big hug before I left and told him I loved him. All of us are devastated by the way this thing went down. I have more respect for him now than I ever did. He didn't deserve this. The world lost a great man."

Conlan was among the football players who served as honor guards in two-man shifts on Tuesday as tens of thousands of mourners filed into the worship room of Pasquerilla Spiritual Center, an interfaith gathering place on campus that had benefited from a $1 million contribution by the Paterno family. White roses sat atop Paterno's undraped casket. Twelve white candles burned in the background. A black-and-white portrait of a smiling Paterno was hung just off to the side. The family arrived first to have a private moment. Joining them was the university's new football coach, Bill O'Brien, who had been hired from the staff of the Super Bowl-bound New England Patriots. Like Paterno, O'Brien had attended Brown University. The football family came next. Members of Paterno's last team arrived in blue university buses, the same ones they took to Beaver Stadium on game days. Among the former players who came to pay final respects was Mike McQueary, who had sat at Paterno's kitchen table in 2002 to tell his boss that he had seen Sandusky sexually assaulting a ten-year-old boy in the showers of the Lasch Building. McQueary entered and exited the spiritual center without speaking to anyone. Then the doors opened to the public. A line of mourners stretched for a quarter of a mile. For some, the wait to view the casket was nearly two hours. An estimated 27,000 mourners passed by the casket during the ten-hour vigil.

On Wednesday a private Roman Catholic Funeral Mass was held inside the spiritual center, located not far from the campus library that bears Paterno's name. A family spokesman said Paterno's grandchildren escorted the casket down the aisle during the opening procession. Among the nonfamily members attending the service was Tim Curley. When the mass was over, pallbearers, including two of Paterno's three sons, Scott and Jay, lifted the casket to begin JoePa's final journey. The casket was gently placed into the back of a hearse painted in Penn State blue.

Family and close friends boarded blue Penn State football buses to take part in a funeral procession that would roll through State College. JoePa always sat in the right front seat of the first bus on game days; this time that seat was occupied by his wife. Moving slowly, the motorcade drove by Beaver Stadium to near the Paterno statue, now overflowing with mementoes. Along with the little stuffed lion Kim and Jonathan Gasper had placed at the monument was a rewritten newspaper headline. The word "FIRED" had been crossed out and replaced with the words "Killed by Trustees." Hundreds of spectators rolled up their trouser cuffs to expose black shoes. Inside the football stadium, the electronic scoreboard was lit up with the image of a smiling Joe Paterno. At the place called Paternoville, the makeshift camp where students slept in tents to get the best seats for football games, students held a sign that said, "We Are Because You Were." The procession proceeded to College Avenue, the main artery in State College, where people stood ten to twenty deep along the sidewalks. The thumping blades of news helicopters could be heard overhead. Some mourners stepped out to touch the blue hearse. Every shop, restaurant, and tavern had a Paterno tribute in the window. On a wall of the Student Book Store at Heister Street a yellow halo was painted above Paterno's image adorning Michael Pilato's mural *Inspiration*. On the far side of the avenue across from the Penn State engineering building, which is constructed in the shape of a slide rule, Moyer's Jewelers had a sign on its building that said, "Happy Valley Welcomes Coach O'Brien."

An estimated 38,000 well-wishers—more than the population of the town—lined College Avenue in response to a Facebook posting to "Guide Joe Paterno Home." Jay Paterno tweeted a message on Twitter that said, "Thank you to all the people who turned out for my father's procession. Very moving." The motorcade proceeded to Pine Hall Cemetery, where the casket, in a private ceremony, was lowered into the soil of a grieving valley.

A public service called "A Memorial to Joe" was held Thursday at the Bryce Jordan Center, where Penn State plays its basketball games and stages music concerts. Cardboard cutouts of Paterno's figure, called "Stand-up Joes," greeted the 12,000 mourners as they entered. A who's who of Penn State dignitaries quietly found their places among the blue and white folding chairs set up on the arena floor while others filled the stands. Hugs were exchanged. Tears flowed. A hush set a solemn tone. It was the quietest the arena had been for any event.

Then Sue Paterno, a picture of grace under pressure, entered the arena from the left. An ovation shattered the silence and then grew in intensity as the throng realized she was in the room. She paused to hug her five children, their spouses, and her seventeen grandchildren before taking her seat.

The memorial began with a video tribute to Paterno that was shown on the scoreboard's giant TV screens. The montage of good times was put together by Guido D'Elia, Penn State's director for communications and branding. D'Elia, head of a Pittsburgh consulting firm called Mind Over Media, had been hired by Penn State with Paterno's blessing to burnish the school's image. He was in control of the on-campus message about Paterno's legacy, and his version, reverent and sanitized, showed moments of football glory and footage of Paterno mingling with adoring fans.

The most heartfelt part of the program was provided by players representing each of the decades in Paterno's long coaching career. Among those to take center stage was Charles V. Pittman, the first African American recruited to play football at Penn State and one of the first participants in Paterno's Grand Experiment stressing academic and athletic excellence. A newspaper publisher and a member of the board of directors of the Associated Press, Pittman spoke as his son, Tony, who also played football under Paterno, sat in the audience with former teammates.

"Joe worked hard to recruit me at Penn State and it seemed, through my young eyes, that he worked ever harder to break my spirit. Nothing seemed good enough for him. He pushed me so hard that he once had me in tears. I called my parents my sophomore year and told them I wanted to come home. My father talked me out of that one," Pittman said, eliciting laughter from his rapt audience.

"What I know now is that Joe wasn't trying to build perfection. That doesn't exist and he knew it. He was, bit by bit, building a habit of excellence. He was building a proud program for the school, the state and the hundreds of young men he watched over for a half century. He cherished honesty, effort, academics, sportsmanship and citizenship. I was forged from that crucible, from Joe's Grand Experiment, and I think the life I have lived is one of Joe's thousands of gifts to the world. Like Joe, many of his former players have tried to make society better in the way that we can.

"Joe made his program his second family—thank you, Sue, for sharing him with us—and family brings comfort. Family survives hard times. It outlasts controversy. Our Penn State family has always lived by Joe's edict that you take care of the little things and the big things will take care of themselves. That is not gone and it will not go away simply because the architect is no longer here. Joe built something fine and good and long lasting and I am humbled by the good fortune of having known him as a coach and a friend. My son, Tony, was so impressed by Joe that he turned down Harvard, Yale and Princeton so he could play football for Coach Joe Paterno." Pittman paused and asked Tony to stand. "That's my boy," he said.

"So now with grown children, grandkids and forty-two years removed from my playing days, I thought Joe Paterno had taught me all that he could teach me. I was wrong. Despite being pushed away from his beloved game and under the extreme pressure of the events of the past few months, Joe's grace was startling. Though his body eventually failed, his spirit never did. Like the great teacher he was all of his life, he had one more lesson for me. I got the call that he passed away on my birthday. What an omen. For me, it means that there is still much to do in this world and those who believed and still believe in Joe's spirit must continue that Grand Experiment. It is needed now, more than ever. Rest in peace, Coach. We'll take it from here."

Michael Robinson, a Penn Stater who is a fullback with the Seattle Seahawks, took an eleven-hour flight from the Pro Bowl in Honolulu to speak at the memorial. What Paterno taught his players will live on, Robinson said. "Just because he's not with us, don't let the dream, don't let the experiment, don't let the values go away. He's in all of us." Robinson returned to Hawaii the next day on Nike Inc.'s corporate jet.

The seminal moment was provided by Phil Knight, the founder and chief executive officer of Nike, a corporate sponsor of the Penn State football program and a donor to the Paterno Library. Knight regaled the audience with anecdotes, telling the story of the time a straitlaced Joe Paterno got up at a Nike-sponsored coaches conference to sing *Wild Thing* by the Troggs, a 1960s rock band that most assuredly did not have a lead singer with a Brooklyn accent. Knight called Paterno his hero, and he took it upon himself to address the issue of whether Paterno may have met his legal but not his moral responsibilities in the Sandusky investigation. Playing the role of a character witness in the court of public opinion, Knight said of Paterno, "He gave full disclosure to his superiors, information that went up the chain to the head of the campus police and the president of the school. The matter was in the hands of a world-class university, and by a president with an outstanding national reputation. Whatever the details of the investigation, this much is clear to me: If there is a villain in this tragedy, it lies in that investigation and not in Joe Paterno's response." Knight's remarks triggered the loudest applause of the memorial. When the ovation died down, Knight asked rhetorically, "Who is the real trustee at Penn State University?"

Some of the speakers had no direct connection to Penn State's football program, but they still had words of praise for Paterno. Lauren Perrotti said she was able to enhance her education and study abroad because she had been chosen to participate in the Paterno Liberal Arts Undergraduate Fellows Program, which had been created by donations made to the school by the coach. "The Paterno Way has become the Penn State Way, and Success with Honor has become the standard," Perrotti said. Also lending his voice to the memorial was Jeff Bast, the original mayor of Paternoville. He said Paterno had influenced every student at Penn State. "JoePa, thank you for being a father to all of us."

The last word belonged to Jay Paterno, the grieving son who served for seventeen years on his father's coaching staff, including the last twelve years as quarterbacks coach. Greeted with a standing ovation, Jay imitated his father's high-pitched Brooklyn accent when he told the audience "Sit down! Sit down!" In his remarks Jay said he was proud that the name on his driver's license is Joseph Vincent Paterno Jr. He quoted Socrates, one of his father's favorite philosophers, that one must wait until evening to see how magnificent the day has been. The line that evoked the warmest applause was when Jay said "Joe Paterno left this world with a clear conscience."

Jay said he once asked his father why, after every football game, he knelt down with his players and joined hands to recite the Lord's Prayer. His father replied that he did so because all of the first-person pronouns in the prayer were plural, "our" and "us," not the singular "I." Jay then asked everyone in the arena to stand and hold hands to say one final prayer in honor of the coach.

"Our Father, who art in heaven, hallowed be thy name," Jay began. "Thy kingdom come, thy will be done, on earth as it is in heaven. Give us this day our daily bread"—Jay's voice broke for a moment—"and forgive us our trespasses, as we forgive those who trespass against us. And lead us not into temptation, but deliver us from evil, for thine is the kingdom, the power, and the glory, forever and ever. Amen."

Jay closed by sharing the last words he spoke at his father's death bed. After a final kiss, he whispered into his father's ear, "Dad, you won. You did all you could do. You've done enough. We all love you. We won. You can go home now."

At that moment Kurt Cleckner, a senior in the Penn State Blue Band, put his lips to the mouthpiece of his trumpet and, standing arrow straight, flawlessly played the school's fight song, "Hail to the Lion." SuePa wept.

After the final note was sounded, a music video appeared on the scoreboard. It was Luciano Pavarotti's spine-tingling rendition of the aria from the final act of Puccini's opera *Turandot*. The final words of the song, translated from Italian, are "I will win! I will win! I will win!"

Through the ordeal of the previous two and a half months Joe Paterno had been denied a grand send-off that his loyal supporters felt he was due. He didn't know at the time that the game of October 29, 2011, the 409th win of his career, would be his last as a coach. Nor that the November 9 practice he watched from his golf cart was his last. The practice ended only hours before he was fired by the board of trustees. But at the conclusion of Pavarotti's aria 12,000 people clapped their hands to acknowledge all the good JoePa had done. Their applause was his final farewell.

The day was clearly reserved for Joe Paterno's memory. Not a single mention was made of the ten young men who were prepared to testify under oath that Jerry Sandusky, counter to his saintly image as a Penn State icon, had sexually abused them over a fifteen-year period. They were not included in any of the prayers. No one spoke on their behalf.

CHAPTER EIGHTEEN

———

CIVIL LAWSUITS

As Jerry Sandusky was slowly receding from the headlines, civil suits began to start pouring in against Sandusky, The Second Mile and Penn State. One was from a twenty-nine-year-old man, who had seen coverage of Sandusky's arrest on network news shows and the cable sports channels. As if in a time machine, he was transported back fifteen years to his time as a Second Mile participant. Then he searched for legal counsel and shared a disturbing secret. He too was one of Jerry's kids, and the time had come to emerge from the shadows. In his own words he wrote a statement for his lawyers to read on his behalf, after they filed the first lawsuit against Sandusky, on November 30, 2011, in Philadelphia.

"I am the man in this lawsuit and I'm writing this statement and taking this action because I don't want other kids to be hurt and abused by Jerry Sandusky or anybody like Penn State to allow people like him to do it—rape kids! I never told anybody what he did to me over 100 times at all kinds of places until the newspapers reported that he had abused other kids and the people at Penn State and Second Mile didn't do the things they should have to protect me and the other kids. I am hurting and have been for a long time because of what happened but feel now even more tormented that I have learned of so many other kids were abused after me. Now that I have told and done something about it I am feeling better and going to get help and work with the police. I want other people who have been hurt to know they can come forward and get help and help protect others in the future." To protect his identity the statement was attributed to John Doe A.

The message was read at a news conference by the attorneys Marci Hamilton of suburban Philadelphia and Jeffrey Anderson of St. Paul, Minnesota, both nationally known experts on cases involving child sex abuse. Their lawsuit listed Sandusky as a defendant, along with The Second Mile Foundation, Penn State University, and others to be named later. It claimed the university and the charity engaged in a conspiracy of silence after incidents of Sandusky's pedophilia were twice reported to them. Their inaction enabled Sandusky to abuse more children for years, according to the suit. The lawsuit sought a minimum of $450,000 in damages, plus interest. A day before filing the lawsuit John Doe A's version of events was turned over to criminal investigators.

For John Doe A, the filing was a cleansing experience. However, he still found it shocking that the grooming he had endured was so similar to the accounts of ten other boys from The Second Mile. According to the lawsuit, John Doe A came from a single-parent household and was living in poverty when he was referred to The Second Mile in 1992, at ten years old and in jeopardy of getting into trouble on the streets. His lawyers would not disclose where he had lived. Things went well for a time, and Sandusky built a trusting relationship with the child's mother. She believed the well-known Penn State defensive coordinator could be the father figure who could save her son from trouble. Thus groomed herself, she encouraged her son to listen to everything Sandusky had to say.

In John Doe A's first year in The Second Mile, Sandusky bestowed gifts and opened doors to worlds he could never imagine. Sandusky took him to Penn State football facilities and Nittany Lions' games, even to one of Penn State's bowl games. In addition, Sandusky took him to football games played by the Philadelphia Eagles.

Then the relationship changed; the fatherly love and affection turned sexual. Favors and gifts came at a huge price, as the mentor began sexually abusing the boy. John Doe A said he was sexually assaulted more than one hundred times from 1992 to 1996. The assaults occurred in Philadelphia, State College, and outside of Pennsylvania when Penn State traveled to a bowl game. Some of the assaults took place in the Penn State football locker rooms and showers. Others happened in the Sandusky home when the boy was invited to sleep over. He wanted to end the abuse, but he was terrified. According to the lawsuit, John Doe A claimed Sandusky said if he ever told a soul about what was going on, he would harm the young man's family. He endured the shame and pain of what was happening because he lived in fear. He suffered in silence.

"He was poor," said Hamilton, his attorney. "Sandusky was the only way he was going to get the kind of attention he was getting, which is typical of a lot of kids."

The lawsuit claimed it could prove that Jerry Sandusky was enabled by Penn State and The Second Mile dating back to the 1970s. From her talks with other lawyers and people familiar with the Sandusky case, Hamilton believes more young people will come forward to tell similar stories. She has successfully litigated cases against the Catholic Church and other religious orders where adults use their authority over children to abuse them, and she said serial child molesters often amass over one hundred victims.

The lawsuit claimed Sandusky was enabled by years of inaction by the two institutions that should have stopped him: "On multiple occasions, Sandusky's interest in, among other things, showering with young boys, and secluding himself alone with boys to permit sexual access to the young boys, was known, or should have been known, to officials with Penn State and Second Mile."

The first warning sign was the 1998 investigation of Sandusky, when Penn State campus police and the state Department of Welfare looked into a complaint by a concerned mother. As described in the lawsuit, "In 1998, an investigation was done into Sandusky's sexually improper conduct with children. . . . Sandusky admitted to showering naked with children at Penn State, admitted to having naked contact in the showers with children and admitted it was wrong of him to do so. Another possible child victim was identified during the investigation. That child was not contacted, and reasonable actions were not taken." The filing noted that Sandusky retired as a coach the following year, but nothing was done to limit his access to Penn State football facilities.

Another opportunity to stop abuse occurred in 2000, when a janitor observed Sandusky assaulting a boy in the Penn State football shower room: "While the janitor immediately informed his direct superior about what he saw, no action was taken and those with information about Sandusky's sexual misconduct with children were discouraged from reporting the incident further."

The suit also claimed a 2002 incident witnessed by Mike McQueary was silenced in a cover-up. After McQueary reported seeing Sandusky sexually assaulting a ten-year-old in the shower at the Lasch Building, Athletic Director Tim Curley and Gary Schultz, the university vice president charged with oversight of the campus police, did little of consequence other than to alert The Second Mile of Sandusky's behavior. "Neither Penn State nor The Second Mile made any other report about the known sexual contact, and neither Penn State nor The Second Mile took any other action to limit Sandusky's access to sexually exploit children, to report Sandusky to law enforcement or to ascertain if Sandusky had molested other children through either Penn State or Second Mile. Had such an investigation been done competently, its results reported, and action taken, both Penn State and Second Mile would have learned that Sandusky had been molesting children since at least the late 1970s and many children after 2002 would not have been sexually assaulted by Sandusky."

Within months of the 2002 report Sandusky turned up as a volunteer football coach at Central Mountain High School in Clinton County, forty miles from State College. Because of a culture of silence at Penn State and The Second Mile, the lawsuit claimed, Sandusky's sexual assaults continued for six more years, until 2008, when a young man at Central Mountain High reported that the coach had abused him for years.

The lawsuit also claimed "significant social and financial links" between Penn State and The Second Mile that may have contributed to the inaction: "Second Mile traded on . . . Sandusky's affiliation with Penn State, its football program, and its revered coach Joe Paterno to increase awareness for its programs and to increase participation by youth. Penn State permitted Second Mile to trade on its image, its reputation, its football program, and its facilities and resources in order to enhance Second Mile's programs and base of donors." Calling the relationship a collaboration, the suit described a series of relationships between Penn State and The Second Mile. They included Paterno's active fundraising efforts for the charity, numerous connections between board members of the charity and university officials, and construction projects at Penn State that provided lucrative contracts for some of The Second Mile's board members.

The lawsuit said John Doe A "has suffered and continues to suffer great pain of mind and body, shock, emotional distress, physical manifestations of emotional distress, embarrassment, loss of self-esteem, disgrace, humiliation and loss of enjoyment of life."

A second lawsuit, also filed in Philadelphia, brought even more troubling accusations against Sandusky, Penn State, and The Second Mile. That suit, filed by attorney Charles Schmidt of Harrisburg shortly after John Doe A's had been filed, said his client was raped in Sandusky's Penn State football office in 2004, when he was one of The Second Miles's summer campers. According to the lawsuit, those events occurred two years after Curley prohibited Sandusky from bringing children to Penn State facilities. Sandusky's attorneys have said he surrendered his keys to the football facilities after he was indicted in November 2011. They assert that the account makes no sense and that it was motivated by possible proceeds from a lawsuit. They did not respond to numerous inquiries for comment.

Several other actions and legal notices have been filed. David Marshall, a lawyer based in Washington, D.C., and a co-counsel for one of the victims, sent letters to child welfare agencies in Centre County requesting that they preserve all records relating to the Sandusky investigation. Letters were also sent to state officials, Curley, Schultz, The Second Mile, and Penn State administrators. In the letters Marshall wrote, "It may have been only Sandusky who laid his hands on these children, but it is clear that a number of other individuals and agencies placed the children in harm's way by knowingly taking actions that allowed the abuse to continue even after they became fully aware of it." Marshall and his team of lawyers, which includes Justine Andronici and Andrew Shubin of State College, represent a young man identified as John Doe in the grand jury presentment and possibly others they have yet to identify.

There are at least ten lawyers awaiting the outcome of Sandusky's criminal prosecution to also file suits against him, Penn State, The Second Mile, and others who might be named in testimony. Under Pennsylvania law there is no hurry. The normal statute of limitations on crime is two years, but in child abuse cases, if the accusers are under the age of eighteen when the crimes occur—as is the case with all of Sandusky's alleged victims who have come forward—they have until they turn thirty to file suit. The first case was filed quickly because the young men had nearly reached the age bar. Lawyers for the rest of the accusers can continue to amass evidence from the criminal prosecution because none of the individuals who claimed abuse has reached the cutoff age.

The only other legal issue that could bar civil actions regards whether or not Penn State and its employees qualify for sovereign immunity under state law. Under that provision, the state and its agencies can't be sued for damages. Immunity is waived when an agent of the state, which would include any Penn State employees embroiled in the scandal, committed crimes during the process.

Lawyers have asked a judge in Centre County to prevent The Second Mile from disbursing any of its assets until the legal issues are settled. Attorney Ben Andreozzi settled a lawsuit with The Second Mile over an injunction he filed to stop it from divesting itself of almost $9 million in assets after the charity agreed to refrain from any such actions until the criminal prosecution unfolded.

Among other legal actions, a former board member of The Second Mile charity sued it over its failure to return $250,000 toward the building of a learning center. Construction for the 45,000-square-foot center was halted after the scandal erupted. As a result Lance Shaner demanded the return of his donations. "We will review the lawsuit and respond appropriately when we have done so, continuing to adhere to our legal responsibilities in the process," said The Second Mile's spokesman Eric Herman in a statement following the suit's filing. "Our primary focus remains helping the children of our communities; we're evaluating the future of our programs so those kids can continue to benefit."

The Second Mile has said it is trying to determine its options. One is to restructure its organization to keep programs going at a reduced level. Another is to transfer its programs to another entity involved in child welfare. Shutting the thirty-five-year-old charity down completely is also on the table. For the moment the charity is closed until further notice. Herman put out a press release in November 2011 expressing sadness and describing the plans going forward: "To this end, we are working with our supporters and partners to let them have a voice in how we move forward. As we do so, the victims and their families will remain foremost in our thoughts and prayers. Ultimately, it is the children who matter."

NOTE: AS THIS BOOK WAS going to press, McKean County senior judge John Cleland ruled to allow Jerry Sandusky, who is under house arrest pending trial, supervised visits with his eleven grandchildren. But the mother of three of those grandchildren, Jill Thomas, said she does not feel comfortable allowing her former father-in-law to see her three sons. "I cannot understand how a court could place the desires of someone who is criminally charged with sexually abusing children above the safety of children," Thomas said in statement released on February 13, 2012.

Thomas is the ex-wife of Sandusky's son, Matthew, with whom she is in a custody battle over her three boys. She claims that her five-year-old son told her that his grandfather had "inappropriately touched" him, but said in a statement that authorities who investigated the allegation told her there was not enough evidence to bring criminal charges.

Thomas said in a statement, "I was also advised . . . that the psychologist who investigated the case had concerns about what had happened to my son and could not rule out that Jerry Sandusky was grooming my son for sexual abuse."

Sandusky's lawyer, Joe Amendola, said the allegations were prompted by the custody battle and were baseless. He hailed the judge's ruling to allow his client visitation with his grandchildren and said Jerry, Dottie, and their family were satisfied with the visitation ruling. "Jerry is also happy he can now have visitation from his longtime friends with prior approval of the Probation Department, and will be able to continue to use the deck to his home to exercise, and care for and supervise his dog, Bo, when Bo is in the yard," Amendola said in a statement after the judge's February 13 ruling.

Neighbors and parents of students who attend the elementary school behind Sandusky's home have voiced concerns that Sandusky seems to be observing the playground when he is outside.

"The commonwealth failed to present any evidence whatsoever that the defendant presents a clearly defined threat to any student at the adjoining elementary school simply by being on his deck," Judge Cleland wrote in his ruling. "No evidence was presented that at any time the defendant made any effort to contact any of the children by signaling or calling to them, or that he made any gestures directed toward them, or that he acted in any inappropriate way whatsoever."

Judge Cleland has said that he is aiming for a May 14, 2012, trial date, although that is considered extremely ambitious due to various legal hurdles that exist before a jury will hear evidence. As far as Jill Thomas and Matt Sandusky's three children are concerned, a legal guardian appointed to represent the interests of the children has submitted a letter to Judge Cleland indicating the boys would like to see their grandfather, but the judge hearing their custody battle will make the decision.

EPILOGUE

Marci Hamilton earned a master's degree in philosophy from Penn State University, but she was more than just an interested alumna as she monitored the memorial service for Coach Joe Paterno. She is a nationally known lawyer who has represented victims of child abuse committed by priests of the Catholic Church and other religious orders, and she represents the client who filed the first civil suit against Jerry Sandusky, The Second Mile, and Penn State.

What stood out in her mind from the January 2012 memorial was that not a single word was said about the young men who have told investigators they were sexually abused by Sandusky. In her view not enough attention had been paid to Paterno's own words, his admission that he wished he had done more in 2002 after Mike McQueary came to him with a disturbing account of a crime against a child. Sadly, Monday-morning quarterbacking was not an option, and the subsequent damage because of the inaction had already been done. "It was very sad that even though everyone at the memorial service was thinking Sandusky and the cover-up, nobody said a word during it," Hamilton said in an interview.

At the memorial's conclusion she posted comments on her Facebook and Twitter accounts to console all survivors of abuse: "Don't feel bad at all. You are not being re-victimized. Many of us are thinking of you. Justice will prevail."

Hamilton said sex abuse victims all over the nation were outraged by Nike founder and CEO Phil Knight's comments defending Joe Paterno. A grassroots movement has begun to boycott Nike gear in response. Among those participating in the boycott are members of the Survivors Network of Those Abused by Priests (SNAP), the oldest and most active nonprofit support group for men and women wounded by religious authority figures. In Hamilton's mind, the insularity at Penn State is similar to the insularity present in the Catholic Church. In that institution, when allegations of abuse where made, the suspected offenders were often removed from the place where the abuse occurred and transferred to a new location, only to abuse again.

Jennifer Storm, the executive director of the Victim/Witness Assistance Program in Harrisburg, is also a Penn State graduate. For two years of her time on campus she lived directly behind Joe Paterno's house in State College and walked by the residence many times on her way to and from campus. One wall in her office in the Dauphin County Courthouse in Harrisburg is adorned with her Penn State diploma and a picture of the Nittany Lion monument. She also monitored the memorial service and found it lacking.

"No one can say that Joe's contributions to Penn State were anything less than admirable and life-changing for many," Storm said. "He made many decisions in his life that led to the betterment of many, and he made one decision that did not. Whether we like it or not, his legacy will forever be intertwined with that one decision he made to not do more. No one is perfect, and no one should be held to the godlike status that Joe was held to by so many of his fans. When we place people high up on pedestals and worship them, we leave them with no place to go but down. We set them and ourselves up for failure. I believe Joe Paterno was a great man, and I believe he made a poor judgment call regarding Jerry Sandusky. I can only hope that the release of that secret was able to bring him ultimate peace and grace in his final days. We're never truly going to know what he knew. He took that to the grave with him. My heart goes out to the faculty members, the workers and the students at Penn State. They didn't ask for this."

Storm has argued in court that the identities of the young men who swore under oath to an investigating grand jury that Sandusky molested them must be kept secret because of the shame and stigma attached to their stories. But part of her job is to speak on behalf of those who have yet to be heard publicly, and she is adamant in her belief that their experiences should not remain in the dark. "Shame and secrecy allow pedophiles to operate," she said.

Storm has written three books dealing with her own experiences. They tell of the wreckage that came after she was raped when she was twelve years old by a man more than twice her age. She spent years trying to bury the shame, turning to alcohol and drugs. Yet she could never rid herself of the ugly burden until she found the courage to speak out. One of her favorite quotes comes from the Irish statesman Edmund Burke, who famously said, "All that is necessary for the triumph of evil is that good men do nothing."

Storm counseled some of the ten young men who were prepared to testify at Sandusky's preliminary hearing before it was waived. From personal experience she knows that they and their families will need counseling to reclaim their lives: "You can have a productive, wonderful life. But there's a place in your soul where it will always exist. You're never beyond it. On some level, it's irreversible. It destroys who you are. A pedophile breaks your spirit and steals your soul. The ending hasn't been written yet. There's a long road ahead for these victims. Everywhere you turn you see the face of your rapist. It never, ever leaves you. It will haunt you for the rest of your life. But with proper therapy and support, you learn to live with it."

What upset her about the memorial and Phil Knight's comments was the missed opportunity to do something for the boys from The Second Mile. Yes, she acknowledged, Penn State has donated a substantial amount of money to create a center for the prevention of child abuse. But those affected most by the Sandusky scandal come from underprivileged families who lack the resources to afford therapy. "I wish they could have done something to provide money for the treatment of the trauma these young men have gone through," Storm said. "If Penn State truly wants to see those boys heal, why not have people donate to a fund to help them with their healing? In a lot of these cases, they don't have enough money to feed their families, let alone get treatment for the trauma they've been through. Some of these young men have families of their own now. Their families need counseling too."

Scant attention has been paid to the ethnicity of the young men, due in part to the steps taken to protect their identities. Lawyers say they are a cross-section of Caucasians and African Americans. Their voices will remain mute until they appear in open court, but according to investigators and attorneys involved in the case, a jury may never get to hear the evidence. Under the most aggressive scheduling imaginable, the earliest date for a trial on the fifty-two charges Sandusky must defend himself against is May 2012, but most likely the trial will be scheduled for 2013. A real possibility exists that more charges will be filed, which would push the schedule back further. Even if only one of the cases results in a conviction, Sandusky, at age sixty-eight, would face prison time for the remainder of his life. A plea bargain is very possible. The negative publicity that would result from having ten or more young men testify in open court may pressure some of the principals to persuade Sandusky to take a plea, but prosecutors will most likely accept a deal only if it costs Sandusky his freedom forever. For now, under the terms of his bail agreement, Sandusky cannot leave his home without court permission. Joseph Amendola, his attorney, has said that Sandusky intends to fight the charges to the bitter end. Amendola has refused to respond to numerous attempts to speak on the matter or to issue a statement on Sandusky's behalf.

The perjury trials of Tim Curley and Gary Schultz are a different matter. Their lawyers are considering separating their cases because the men's circumstances are markedly different. Curley has vehemently denied knowing anything about abuse allegations against Sandusky except for the 2002 incident witnessed by Mike McQueary. He also has health issues; he is being monitored closely by doctors to make sure there has been no recurrence of lung cancer, diagnosed in 2010. Schultz has more legal hurdles than Curley. Not only was he part of the 2002 inquiry, but he was also aware of the 1998 investigation of Sandusky by campus police. Now retired, Schultz could lose his lucrative state pension if convicted of a felony. Pleading to a lesser charge of "failing to report an incident of abuse" is also a possibility for the lifelong employee of Penn State.

McQueary's status remains in limbo. The State College native and former Penn State quarterback was placed on paid administrative leave on November 18, 2011. He could remain on paid leave indefinitely while the case plays out. Sandusky's lawyer has branded McQueary a coward and a liar. Some believe he should have been charged as a co-conspirator because he didn't go directly to the police after the 2002 shower incident. His chances of returning to the sidelines as a coach at Penn State are unlikely. The new head football coach of the Nittany Lions, Bill O'Brien, has already filled out his staff. McQueary has been steadfast in his testimony that he told his superiors that he witnessed a sexual act between Sandusky and a ten-year-old boy, but defense lawyers believe his credibility will be attacked in either the Sandusky case or the perjury cases. Under Pennsylvania's 1986 whistleblower law, Penn State may not be able to fire him. He did report wrongdoing, even though he did not rescue the child or go to state or campus police. The university will have to keep him on the payroll or come up with a mutually acceptable severance package. Whether he coaches again anywhere else is an unknown. It may be hard for him to find a position given his close association with this scandal.

Joe Paterno's son Jay lost his job and his father in less than a month. After seventeen years as an assistant on his father's staff, including twelve years as quarterbacks coach, Jay was not retained by the new regime. He has been the family's lead spokesman since the passing of his father on January 22, 2012, and has been the staunchest defender of his father's legacy. Jay has said he is considering his options, both inside and outside college football. He has resumed writing a column for statecollege.com.

And what of JoePa's legacy? It is undeniable he had enviable graduation rates, donated more money to his university than any other football coach in history, remained a firm believer in academic excellence, and won a record 409 games. In the insular world of Penn State, he will always be an icon for his countless good deeds. But there will always be questions about a morality issue, one sin of omission stemming from a lapse of judgment. He never said what more he wished he would have done or why he didn't do it when McQueary told him about Sandusky. His supporters will always argue that he deserved better than to be fired over the phone. But his name has been erased from the Big Ten Conference championship trophy, so clearly the trend people are following at the moment is to distance themselves.

Sandusky's arrest has tainted the reputation of a first-rate university. Because of his case, colleges and universities across the land are reexamining policies concerning children on campus and their standards for reporting sexual abuse, especially sexual abuse of a minor. Legislatures from Pennsylvania to Louisiana to Oregon are looking into strengthening codes dealing with sex abuse or making it easier for victims to come forward. Federal laws such as the Child Abuse Prevention and Treatment Act may also be strengthened. Sheldon Kennedy, a former National Hockey League player who was sexually abused by the disgraced junior coach Graham James, testified before the U.S. Senate that adults must be educated on how to identify pedophiles to prevent abusers from finding more victims.

Whether Penn State lives up to its promise to be more transparent or reverts to its insular culture remains to be seen. The Penn State family has wounds to heal, and the process will take time. The university has launched its own investigation into the events that transpired and has promised to follow the evidence wherever it leads. The school is also facing probes by the U.S. Department of Education, the NCAA, and the Big Ten Conference, among others.

And what of the young men who, when asked, told investigators they were abused for years? If Jennifer Storm could hold a forum for the survivors of The Second Mile, the topic would be healing and rebuilding trust. Based on her own experience, she cautions that moving forward is a long and painful but necessary journey. "I would acknowledge their bravery in coming forward," Storm said. "I would acknowledge that they did not waiver in the face of intimidation and public scrutiny and public speculation. I would encourage anyone else to come forward—and there are many others who suffered similar abuse—to join the fight for justice and to stop this monster. And I would call for some sort of fund to help them get treatment."

This story remains a tragedy, Storm said. She acknowledged the professionalism of Pennsylvania State Police trooper Joseph Leiter, whose one-man investigation helped to crack the case. But the tragic errors or lapses in judgment made by so many of the supposedly principled characters from Penn State and The Second Mile are inexplicable.

"No one comes out a winner. No one comes out a hero. No one tried to stop the violence," Storm said. "I keep seeing that little boy in the shower. He turns around and sees someone is witnessing what a sexual predator is doing to him. Maybe that witness will do something. Maybe this nightmare will stop. Maybe there will be a knock on the door and it'll be the police and this will all end. Then, when the knock came, it was Jerry again."

Throughout his life Joe Paterno was guided by the story of Aeneas, the mythical figure who left the fallen kingdom of Troy and struggled through adversity to found the new empire of Rome. This character from literature was conflicted over the demands of being a leader, and the gods made him suffer when he tried to avoid his responsibilities. Paterno often referred to this story in his informal sessions with sports writers, saying, "As Aeneas found out, life comes down on you with some terrible whacks if you don't do the right thing." The theme of tragedy has never been more poignant.

Penn State will move forward, even if some of the legacies need to be revised. Jerry Sandusky, Tim Curley, and Gary Schultz await their day in court. Joe Paterno is in eternal rest. The great institution of Penn State University will certainly shine again. As the alma mater proclaims,

May no act of ours bring shame
To one heart that loves thy name.
May our lives swell that fame,
Dear Old State, Dear Old State.

ACKNOWLEDGMENTS

The authors would like to thank Frank Weimann of the Literary Group International, our agent, for championing this project. We are grateful to Lisa Sharkey and Amy Bendell of HarperCollins Publishers for their diligent efforts to bring this work to fruition. We never could have gotten this book completed without the careful and creative editing skills of Lisa Pulitzer and Martha Smith, as well as their dedicated efforts under extreme deadline pressures. The authors thank Michael Fuoco for his support and advice. We also thank our families for their understanding and patience during this arduous process.